SDG9 – INDUSTRY, INNOVATION AND INFRASTRUCTURE

CONCISE GUIDES TO THE UNITED NATIONS SUSTAINABLE DEVELOPMENT GOALS

Series Editors

Walter Leal Filho
World Sustainable Development Research and Transfer Centre, Hamburg University of Applied Sciences

Mark Mifsud
Centre for Environmental Education and Research, University of Malta

This series comprises 17 short books, each examining one of the UN Sustainable Development Goals.

The series provides an integrated assessment of the SDGs from an economic, social, environmental and cultural perspective. Books in the series critically analyse and assess the SDGs from a multi-disciplinary and a multi-regional standpoint, with each title demonstrating innovation in theoretical and empirical analysis, methodology, and application of the SDG concerned.

Titles in this series have a particular focus on the means to implement the SDGs, and each one includes a short introduction to the SDG in question along with a synopsis of their implications on the economic, social, environmental and cultural domains.

SDG9 – INDUSTRY, INNOVATION AND INFRASTRUCTURE

BY

LUIS VELAZQUEZ
University of Sonora, Mexico

United Kingdom – North America – Japan – India
Malaysia – China

Emerald Publishing Limited
Howard House, Wagon Lane, Bingley BD16 1WA, UK

First edition 2022

Reprints and permissions service
Contact: permissions@emeraldinsight.com

British Library Cataloguing in Publication Data
A catalogue record for this book is available from the British Library

ISBN: 978-1-80117-134-2 (Print)
ISBN: 978-1-80117-131-1 (Online)
ISBN: 978-1-80117-133-5 (Epub)

Printed and bound by CPI Group (UK) Ltd, Croydon, CR0 4YY

ISOQAR certified
Management System,
awarded to Emerald
for adherence to
Environmental
standard
ISO 14001:2004.

Certificate Number 1985
ISO 14001

INVESTOR IN PEOPLE

This book is dedicated to my professors, colleagues, former students, family, and friends, all my fellow adventurers on my tireless quest for sustainability. Moreover, I also dedicate it to those students worldwide who will become the agents of change needed to achieve inclusive and sustainable industrialisation and a better world.

CONTENTS

ABOUT THE AUTHOR

Luis Velazquez, PhD, is a Sustainability Senior Sustainability Researcher with over 30 years of experience as an Industrial Engineer. He holds a Doctoral degree in Engineering Science with a major in Cleaner Production and Pollution Prevention from the University of Massachusetts Lowell. He has been a Sustainability Research Intern at several higher education institutions, such as the Center for Health and the Global Environment of the Harvard School of Public Health, Boston, USA; the Paulista University, Sao Paulo, Brazil; Erasmus University, Rotterdam, Holland; and the University of Applied Sciences in Zittau/Görlitz, Germany. Since 1993, he has served as a Project Manager in several sustainability initiatives in different countries. In addition, he has conducted several investigations in the Sustainability, Cleaner Production, and Pollution Prevention fields and the study of sustainable universities.

DISCLAIMER

The views expressed in this book do not reflect the opinions or views of any organisation, agency, or program of the United Nations or any other international agency.

PREFACE

Although *SDG9: Industry, Innovation and Infrastructure* targets students and professors in the field of Engineering Management, it is also intended for those students, professors, researchers, and practitioners in related fields. It has been almost 30 years since I graduated as an industrial engineer from the University of Sonora in Mexico and practically the same time since Sustainable Development captivated me.

My quest for sustainability in the industry has been fascinating and challenging, as I have had successes and disappointments. During these three decades, I have had the opportunity to study sustainability at prestigious universities worldwide. Everything I have experienced has been valuable, but if I had to select the most valuable thing, without a doubt, it is the experiences shared with my colleagues and with students. I have collaborated with sustainability experts in North America, South America, Europe, Asia, Africa, and Arabia; everyone taught me so much about sustainability.

The invitation to write this book came from a researcher in Germany whom I consider an icon of Sustainability Science; however, my most significant spiritual motivation has always been the students. For them, I accepted the invitation, hoping that they will find inspiration to be agents of change and soon help achieve inclusive and sustainable industrialisation. The students have been an injection of enthusiasm and optimism at a most challenging moment of my career; therefore, a reason not to give up. While I do not consider myself a sustainability expert, writing about inclusive and sustainable industrialisation initially did not seem as challenging as it turned out.

The most challenging phase was gathering information about SDG9 because there appears to be a lack of reliable SDG9 information available and what exists is hard to find. The searching for information lasted months and sometimes was frustrating and futile. This fact is likely because progress towards SDG9 has not been as positive as it might be. It is not that the current SDG9 published literature is wrong, but the evidence is not conclusive. In general, though, information sources often offer qualitative information, and quantitative data are scarce. Moreover, there is no trustworthy or go-to source of information that indicates with certainty the progress towards the 2030 Agenda; therefore, generating insights about assessing progress towards the achievement of SDG9 was somewhat difficult; it was like piecing together a puzzle. This situation is not exclusive to SDG9; thus, several of the arguments expressed in the book might apply to multiple SDGs.

In the end, I have managed to present a comprehensive framework within which complex SDG9 issues can be understood to be adapted and applied effectively and efficiently in particular situations. Therefore, I hope that this book helps build qualified human resources to accelerate progress towards SDG9 by increasing awareness and knowledge towards a low-carbon and inclusive industrialisation.

ACKNOWLEDGEMENTS

I express my most profound appreciation to Dr Walter Leal Filho, Director of the Research and Transfer Centre 'Sustainability Development and Climate Change Management', Chair of Climate Change Management at the Hamburg University of Applied Sciences in Germany, and Chair of Environment and Technology at Manchester Metropolitan University in the United Kingdom for his kind invitation, and trust, to write this book. I also want to thank professor Mark C. Mifsud from the University of Malta for this invitation.

I am entirely indebted to my colleague Krystal Perkins, from the Department of Psychology, School of Natural and Social Sciences, Purchase College, SUNY, USA, for her support, inspiration, and guidance during the writing process. I would also like to acknowledge my colleagues in the Sustainability Graduate Program of the University of Sonora, who had helped me tune up the book's content.

Finally, yet importantly, I would like to thank my lovely family and friends for their patient and understanding during the months I spent writing the book.

INTRODUCTION

There is nothing more attractive for students committed to sustainability than becoming agents of change for their community, country, or, why not, the world. To achieve that dream, the sacrifices that have to be made, the hours of study, sleeplessness, and even disappointments do not matter. To enhance their learning experience, the purpose of this book is twofold: to present and debate the relevant body of SDG9 literature with a particular focus on U.N. documents and explore the fascinating and cross-cutting aspects that jeopardise achieving SDG9 Industry, innovation, and infrastructure.

This book is addressed to talented bachelor and postgraduate students and professors in the field of Engineering Management or closely related academic programs. For them, contributing to the consolidation of inclusive and sustainable industrialisation should be the highest aspiration in their professional life.

The U.N. 2030 Agenda aims to meet 17 sustainability goals by 2030. Still, SDG9 is the most significant for all industry sectors because it seeks new steps towards inclusive and sustainable industrialisation. For the U.N., visioning, inclusive, and sustainable industrialisation had been a recurrent ambition since, the World Summit on Sustainable Development, better known as the Earth Summit, was held in Rio de Janeiro almost thirty years ago.

However, the U.N.'s insistence on fostering inclusive and sustainable industrialisation has not rendered the expected results. Outcomes so far are, to say at least, disappointing. Worse, the COVID-19 pandemic has exacerbated conditions in almost all sectors, especially in industrial settings, which has further complicated the future achievements towards SDG9.

The first chapter starts with an overview of the fundamental concepts to better understand SDG9 and its targets. Then, the importance of issues like resilient infrastructure, technological innovation, information and communications technology, inclusive and sustainable industrialisation, and financial services are debated to gain valuable insights on SDG9.

The second chapter presents a detailed analysis to understand how member states' delegations report the progress made in implementing the Sustainable Development Goals (SDGs) and targets as mandated in the A/RES/70/1 Resolution. In this chapter, students will have the opportunity to review U.N. landmark events from which the 2030 Agenda emerged. Then, students will be able to delve into the guidance documents issued by the U.N. High-level Political Forum on Sustainable Development (HLPF) for reviewing individual countries' progress. The most controversial issue covered in this chapter undoubtedly concerns information gathering. The chapter also covers the guidelines of two independent external organisations, such as the Global Compact Initiative and Global Reporting Initiative used by firms to legitimate sustainability reporting content and increase reliability. The chapter concludes with a brief description of required procedures to submit and present Voluntary National Reviews (VNRs).

The purpose of the third chapter is to examine factors involved in reporting and other critical issues necessary to understand the progress and how we are progressing towards SDG9. From this point on, data for our debate comes mainly from U.N. sources such as the 2017 High-level Political Forum on Sustainable Development and the Sustainable Development Goals Report 2020. The official information is complemented with independent assessments of 2020 VNRs, other SDGs reports, and scientific literature.

The last chapter covers the Decade of Action to improve actual efforts to accomplish the 2030 Agenda. The industry would undoubtedly play an essential role in supporting this call; however, for this to be possible, it will first have recover from the effects of the pandemic. This chapter illustrates the adverse impacts that the construction, manufacturing, and hospitality industries have suffered since the beginning of the COVID-19 pandemic and how they gradually have returned to the new normal. The chapter also shows the case of the industry that could be considered the 'champion in the COVID era', the high-tech industry. Finally, the book is closed with an invitation to *Build Back Better Together,* reflecting on the fundamental principle of SDG9, which is sustainable industrialisation, but above all, inclusivity. The SDG9 cannot be considered achieved until its benefits are transferred to the countries in the global south.

1

THE FUNDAMENTAL CONCEPTS OF SDG9

ABSTRACT

The 2030 United Nations Agenda has framed Sustainable Development Goal 9 around eight targets outlined in Resolution A/RES/71/313 (U.N. General Assembly, 2017). The purpose of this chapter is that the lectors, without much previous knowledge on SDG9, understand the fundamental concepts involved in each of the eight targets. Multiple discussion points emerge when reflecting on the nature of these concepts and others emerge when reflecting on them in the industry settings. The first section of this chapter covers issues concerning resilient infrastructure. Resilient infrastructure is related to targets 9.1, 9.4, and 9.a. This concept needs to cope with extreme natural events potentially associated with global warming and climate change. The second section focusses on the importance of technological innovation in the context of targets 9.5 and 9.b. In a business domain, innovation allows to strengthen industrial competitiveness and increases corporate sustainability. The third concept covered in this chapter is the Information and

Communication Technology that is a key to understand target 9.c. Last but not the least, two essential ideas are discussed: Inclusive and sustainable industrialisation and financial services, which are fundamental elements in target 9.2 and target 9.3. In a certain way, it is possible to conclude that both concepts integrate all previous conceptions.

Keywords: Resilient infrastructure; innovation; information and communication technology; inclusive and sustainable industrialisation; financial services; SDG9

Within the 2030 Agenda, SDG9 is one of the most important, if not the most important, for the industry and, therefore, for a country's inclusive and sustainable development and growth. In the following sections, each of the fundamental concepts and terms is broken down to understand this objective.

1.1. RESILIENT INFRASTRUCTURE

Resilient infrastructure is one of the most complicated ideas for students to understand. This concept involves a significant amount of subjectivity when deciding upon the level of resilience. The idea of resilient infrastructure relates to the following SDG9's targets:

> *TARGET 9.1: Develop quality, reliable, sustainable, and resilient infrastructure, including regional and trans-border infrastructure, to support economic development and human well-being, with a focus on affordable and equitable access for all. (U.N. General Assembly, 2017)*

> *TARGET 9.4: By 2030, upgrade infrastructure and retrofit industries to make them sustainable, with increased resource-use efficiency and greater adoption of clean and environmentally sound technologies and industrial processes, with all countries taking action*

> *in accordance with their respective capabilities. (U.N. General Assembly, 2017)*
>
> *TARGET 9.a: Facilitate sustainable and resilient infrastructure development in developing countries through enhanced financial, technological, and technical support to African countries, least developed countries, landlocked developing countries and small island developing States. (U.N. General Assembly, 2017)*

There are many factors to be considered in understanding what resilient infrastructure is; for instance, infrastructure can be climate-resilient but fragile to fire, earthquakes, or floods. Let us start with the basics; infrastructure refers to an entity's physical structure such as firm, city, region, or country. On the other hand, resilience is the capability to recover from or adjust to change, whatever the cause, in the shortest period possible. While no standard definition of the term resilient infrastructure exists across various disciplines, in sustainability, the term strongly relates to the system's capacity to return to its original sustainability level before a natural disaster (Chatterjee & Layton, 2020).

Concerning this approach, Helmrich et al. (2020) conceptualise a resilient infrastructure system as resilient to numerous potential disturbances, not only natural disasters, by adopting 'Life's Principles' associated with the resilience in ecological systems. On the other hand, from an engineering approach, resilience is understood as the structural integrity of systems and physical infrastructure, essential to ensure continued operational performance during extreme loading (EOD Resilience Resources, 2016). Therefore, other anthropogenic potential disturbances can be caused by human error, such as fires, explosions, etc. The essential rationality of integrating ecological principles in industrial settings is not new; it gained popularity by the mid-nineties with the emergence of industrial ecology.

For Industrial Ecology scholars, natural and industrial systems are intrinsically interconnected and mutually reinforcing, particularly regarding resources and industrial growth where competition and cooperation are present in a balanced way (Ehrenfeld, 2000; Tilley, 2003).

Similarly, the relationship between sustainability and resilient infrastructure has to be found in both directions. That is to say; sustainability can influence the infrastructure's resilience and vice versa; a resilient infrastructure can determine the sustainability of a system (Gromek & Sobolewski, 2020). During extreme weather conditions, accidents, and natural disasters, infrastructure systems are highly vulnerable. This situation is particularly critical in climate change-related events because it is a matter of life and death in many of the emerging countries of the Global South (Chirisa, Bandauko, Mazhindu, Kwangwama, & Chikowore, 2016).

Building resilient infrastructure is not enough to warrant the resilience of systems. The governance of resilient infrastructure is another vital component to strengthening countries' productivity and competitiveness (Huck, Monstadt, Driessen, & Rudolph-Cleff, 2021). At least, private participation in building infrastructure and its governance has always been controversial (Baker, Khater, & Haddad, 2019). The debate heats up for critical infrastructures such as those related to electricity, gas, and water (MacArthur, Hoicka, Castleden, Das, & Lieu, 2020; Spencer & Meng, 2019). On the other hand, middle-income and lower-income countries currently spend many funds to procure and administer COVID-19 vaccines that they might have no choice but support the crowding-in of private investment. However, it can no longer be taken for granted. According to a novel World Bank Infrastructure report, the worldwide private investment in infrastructure decreased by 56% during the first months of the COVID-19 pandemic compared to investment levels in the first half-year of 2019 (The World Bank, 2020).

In response to these developments, sustainability technologists find the design of lower-carbon and climate-resilient infrastructure indispensable to respond and recover from extreme events as fast as possible. The broad spectrum of resilient technologies covers from tear-resistant and self-healing concrete material for construction (Zhang, Zheng, Ashour, & Han, 2020) to autonomous and disaster-resistant infrastructures through integrating cognitive and self-deployable load-bearing structural components (Naser, 2019). Furthermore, modern information technologies focus on developing co-optimization algorithms to optimise urban energy systems and interconnected urban infrastructures affected by urban morphology to increase climate resilience (Perera, Javanroodi, & Vahid, 2021). Finally, the monitoring of critical infrastructure systems related to the generation and supply of electricity, gas, and water must be carried out early if its continuous operation is compromised. Hence, the role of technical specialists with knowledge of specific technical issues is a decisive factor in ensuring that technical failures and accidents under stressful operation conditions will not undermine the system's resilience (Chang, Mcdaniels, Fox, Dhariwal, & Longstaff, 2014).

The following section presents a real-world illustrative case to depict the severe consequences of failing in building resilient infrastructure.

- Illustrative case study

Critical infrastructure systems are tried out to the uttermost when natural disasters occur. In such circumstances, it is expected that the infrastructure system runs smoothly with no failures. Regrettably, our case study illustrates the 'calvary' of Texas citizens due to a severe winter storm during February 2021. This case shows a real-life situation in which more than four million households in Texas spent hours, and some of them spent days without electricity, gas, and drinkable water because of the poor resilience in the Texan electric grid infrastructure system (Practical Engineering, 2021).

By February 2021, the freezing temperature of a winter storm turned off the power-generating facilities in Texas, including those fuelled by natural gas, coal, wind, and nuclear power. In response, the Electric Reliability Council of Texas, the agency that governs the electric grid in the state, instituted lengthy rolling blackouts to prevent high electricity demand from exceeding supply (Fanning, Ament, & Brisbin, 2021). CNN pictured this situation as a warning that could be the new normal nationwide because of climate change (CNN, 2021). When electricity was restored, Texans faced problems such as pipes bursting and taps running dry, leaving them in deplorable conditions (Blunt & Passy, 2021). In addition, the cost of electricity skyrocketed on variable-rate electricity plans users, something that Texas's governor considered unacceptable (Firozi, 2021). Then, politicians took the electricity infrastructure debate out of the infrastructure context and started to fuel a party-political dispute by blaming each other (Bendix, 2021). So far, there have been some governance-related disputes between the federal government and the state authorities that debated the need to establish winterisation requirements, energy storage resources, and transmission infrastructure, but relevant changes in Texan's legislation are unlikely to take place (Melvin, 2021). In the meantime, the state's attorney general authorised the suspension of energy bills triggering legal struggles and civil lawsuits in federal bankruptcy courts, state courts, and the Texas legislature (Englund, 2021).

The negative consequences did not end in Texas territory; the lack of natural gas escalated into a two-nation problem that affected the entire region between the United States and Mexico when the Texas Governor banned gas shipping out of the state's border. This mandate caused diplomatic conflict between both countries (Carroll, Blas, & Dlouhy, 2021). The suspension of gas exportation to Mexico had an enormous impact on millions of electricity consumers in many Mexican states and hundreds of factories that had to shut down operations, losing billions of dollars due to rolling blackouts (Angulo & Barrera, 2021). This sequence of unfortunate events, and its consequences, could have been avoided if the grid infrastructure had been resilient to frigid winter weather. Unfortunately, Texan's electric grid was not conditioned for such weather conditions (Smith, 2021).

This previous Texan's illustrative case supports the importance of building resilient infrastructure to avoid people's suffering, the affections on industries, and the development of countries. Slowly, the region is recovering from this catastrophic event. The case study explores several lessons drawn from the bitter experience in Texas that can inform about the severe consequences of poor resilient infrastructure. The key lessons included the importance of fostering resilient infrastructure and the significance of responding late to extreme climatological events. Furthermore, building and governing resilient infrastructure is a critical component for countries' economic growth because a failure in its operation could negatively impact the safety and security of society, its environment and compromise its future.

The following concept addressing in this chapter is innovation. Along with resilient infrastructure, innovation is at the core of SDG9.

1.2. INNOVATION

Marketing and advertising by firms daily bombard us with multiple strategies that include the word 'innovation'. Customers find the word innovation everywhere, from media ads to cybernetic banners, streaming services, and more. On a national scale, countries have a strong interest in increasing their national innovation capacity to boost economic development and growth (Kayal, 2008). At a glance, innovation relates to new products, services, processes, procedures, inclusive ideas, but in sustainability industrial settings, the concept is more complex than it sounds. Without a strong innovation capacity, it will not be possible for countries to meet SDG9 (Szopik-Depczyńska et al., 2018). Therefore, the conceptualisation of innovation is vital to the understanding of the following targets:

> *TARGET 9.5: Enhance scientific research, upgrade the technological capabilities of industrial sectors in all countries, in particular developing countries, including, by 2030, encouraging innovation and substantially increasing the number of research and development workers per 1 million people and public and private research and development spending. (U.N. General Assembly, 2017)*

> *TARGET 9.b: Support domestic technology development, research, and innovation in developing countries, including by ensuring a conducive policy environment for, inter alia, industrial diversification and value addition to commodities. (U.N. General Assembly, 2017)*

In this matter, the National Innovation System (NIS) concept has been widely accepted since it aims to improve the efficiency of production processes and, consequently, strengthen industrial competitiveness, although mostly in industrialised countries (Afzal, Lawrey, & Gope, 2019). Zhang (2019) summarises the contributions of the national innovation system framework as follows; the first contribution is the attention paid to increase international competitiveness through innovation. The second contribution is the differentiation between dramatic and marginal innovation. Finally, it broadens the analysis of innovation to include aspects of national capacity beyond the business focus. The last contribution is the most significant because it intrinsically highlights the vital role of federal innovation regulators, which coordinate the efforts undertaken by each participant within the innovation system, such as firms, higher

education institutions, investors, lawyers, and other stakeholders (Binz & Truffer, 2017). In this regard, scholars interested in
developing new sustainable innovations often stress the importance of fostering supportive system resources among research
and development stakeholders (Calabrese, Castaldi, Forte, &
Levialdi, 2018; Musiolik, Markard, & Hekkert, 2012).

Much of the innovation in large firms is driven by the desire
to increase their number of patents. In contrast, expanding the
number of publications is the most common drive (Schwartz,
Peglow, Fritsch, & Günther, 2012). For small firms and individual inventors, patents are means to access national funds
to consolidate or start a business (Veer & Jell, 2012). A controversial innovation drive is a cross-industry innovation. This
innovation mode refers to the transfer of knowledge used to
innovate something in one industrial sector to another industry
or business to improve its current process, product, or service or
develop a new design. This phenomenon can occur by worker
interaction via job turnover or personal relationships (Enkel &
Gassmann, 2010). In truth, the legality of this method can be
disputed by intellectual property rights (IPR) and competition
laws, which guarantee that the revenue from innovation goes to
patent holders. The other side of the coin happens when patents
become a tool for unethical, fraudulent, or corrupt marketing
practices (Stakheyeva, 2018). However, this is another story.

On an industry scale, designers are currently facing the
demand from the society that all technological innovation be
conceptualised, taking into account contributing to achieving
the SDGs by providing benefits to low-income communities,
preferentially, in the Global South (Hostettler, 2018). Encouraging involvement in innovation programs closely related to
social concerns is not easy for firms and usually requires partnership with governmental agencies. For instance, the European
Union (E.U.) introduced a new international policy agenda that
includes the European Commission Horizon 2020 research and

innovation program (Biggi & Giuliani, 2021). In this program, the European Commission (E.C.) defines Responsible Research and Innovation as '*the approach that anticipates and assesses potential implications and societal expectations about concerning research, and innovation, to foster the design of inclusive and sustainable research and innovation*' (European Commission, 2020). Together with corporate social responsibility (CSR), responsible innovation might jointly improve the bottom line from conceptualising the idea. However, it is necessary to be aware that tools for responsible innovation are borrowed from research centres, and the development of specific tools for industry business is still in its infancy (Jarmai, 2020).

The picture is different from the environmental dimension of sustainable development. Firms have created innovative solutions to respond to society's concerns to prevent severe consequences from non-renewable energy sources, industrial chemicals, and the production of massive non-recyclable waste (Lim & Sonko, 2019). In this sense, environmental law has become a driver to design new sustainability solutions to environmental problems (Freeman, 2017) while obtaining economic benefits (Lanfranchi, 2010). The adoption of cleaner production technology has improved the eco-efficiency of industrial processes, resulting in a more robust business innovation capacity to reduce carbon footprint, waste, emissions, and pollutants (Bhupendra & Sangle, 2015). Environmental tools such as Design for Environment (DfE) are based on life-cycle thinking that increases chances to reduce the ecological burden on ecosystems and populations and drives innovation (Romeo, 2010). Innovations in the form of DfE have been on the radar of sustainability stakeholders for more than two decades (Wiesmeth, 2020). Nowadays, a growing body of evidence from both academia and practitioners supports the strong relationship between DfE and Quality Management Innovation (QMI) to enhance environmental and economic performance (Jackson, Gopalakrishna-Remani, Mishra, & Napier, 2016).

Most technological innovations start being pilot projects in a research centre or university to transfer to private industry. However, in the context of the 2030 agenda, there is a growing concern that technological innovations do not benefit countries in the Global South; worse yet, a more significant matter is how to help the poorest countries to build their innovation and technological capacity. Whether resilient technology is designed to protect people, conserve natural resources, or reduce pollution, it needs to be transferred into lower-income countries. For example, governments have supported innovative technology to prevent and protect vulnerable people from natural disasters in response to that issue. Indeed, technology transfer strategies might enable countries to effectively address SDG9, as long as participatory technology approaches are considered to keep the rights of all actors in searching for their innovative solutions. Of course, the predominant route for technology transfer during decades has been from north to south. Yet, a new path for technology transfer and cooperation is emerging from south-to-south countries (Kirchherr & Urban, 2018).

Resilient technologies penetrate technology markets to address low-carbon climate change-related events and foster a low-carbon future (Golz, 2016; Kennedy & Corfee-morlot, 2013). Perhaps, they are not far from staying at the forefront of technology; however, one might say that the great challenge countries collectively face is not leaving anyone behind. The decade from action invites everybody, at all levels, to accelerate a sustainable solution to meet the SDGs. Concerning SDG9, it is necessary to move forwards to responsible innovation at a faster pace. An essential factor of responsible innovation is linked to Information and Communication Technology (ICT); in this context, the following section covers the information and communication technology industry at the core of inclusive and sustainable industrial development.

1.3. INFORMATION AND COMMUNICATION TECHNOLOGY

This section encompasses the discussion about the fundamental concepts to understand how to meet the following target:

TARGET 9.c: Significantly increase access to information and communications technology and strive to provide universal and affordable access to the Internet in the least developed countries by 2020. (U.N. General Assembly, 2017)

ICT is one of the cornerstones of a new fundamental paradigm of industrial production, better known as Industry 4.0, that focusses on advanced digitalisation within factories (Lasi, Fettke, Feld, & Hoffmann, 2014). The contribution of ICT regarding SDG9 is vast and diverse in many respects (ITU & UN-OHRLLS, 2018). Hopefully, the adoption of the advancement of Industry 4.0 technologies such as Cyber-Physical Systems (CPS), Internet of Things (IoT), and Big Manufacturing Data Analytics, companies across all sectors should catalyse the progress towards industry sustainability (Wang & Xu, 2019). However, the extent and speed to which ICT can accelerate firms' progress towards SDG9, and all sets of SDGs, would depend on the corporate sustainability vision, mission, goals, and targets for each business or industry (Ghobakhloo, 2018). For instance, digital technology and the IoT have stepped up the value chain from operational data of a large set of vehicles and heavy-duty industrial equipment in the logistic manufacturing sector while reducing fuel cost and CO_2 emissions (Pashkevich, Haftor, Karlsson, & Chowdhury, 2019). Likewise, ICT software and appliances have enhanced energy-efficient strategies to improve production processes (Hilty et al., 2006). Industry 4.0 is characterised by smart-oriented digital solutions to break down industrial constraints and contribute to value creation.

This characteristic may lead to false inferences and conclude that Industry 4.0 is exclusive to firms with large-scale infrastructure projects that require highly automated computerised systems (Hetemi, Ordieres-Meré, & Nuur, 2020). However, this perspective is wrong because ICT is also helpful and affordable for Small and Medium Enterprises (SMEs) in their quest for Industry 4.0 (Amaral & Peças, 2021).

We need to be aware that, in some instances, there are trade-offs involved with the arrival of IoT in the industry, such as the potential disruptions of the environment, natural resources, and health due to the obsolete replacing equipment such as computers, appliances, wires, etc. That is why government authorities, at the national, state, and municipal levels, must be prepared to foster e-waste management strategies that range from toxic use reduction techniques to new developments in policy and legislation (Niu, et al., 2021; Ottoni, Dias, & Xavier, 2020; Patil & Ramakrishna, 2020). The incorporation of IoT into the industry demands the involvement of public authorities in establishing new rules for electrical or electronic equipment that has been discarded, also calls as e-waste. However, creating new legal frameworks requires the consensus of many political interests and, therefore, time to develop. So far, a great deal is to be done regarding public management strategies to reduce pollution from electronic sources (Pedro, Giglio, Velazquez, & Munguia, 2021; Wang, Kong, Li, Li, & Wang, 2020) and protect public and occupational health (Velázquez, et al., 2008).

The ICT domain or system is transforming the production process primarily to increase productivity while improving the safety condition of workers by reducing unintentional human errors resulting from poor judgement, lack of knowledge, or bad applications (Angelopoulou, Mykoniatis, & Boyapati, 2020). Still, ironically, the replacement of workers by machines can result in job losses (Benitez, et al., 2021). Thus, the interaction between ICT technology and humans had diversified the work environment. Still, it is expected that shortly, in most cases, human interaction with machines will not exist in ICT environments. Although it is also true that the advent of technology in the industry will require new profiles of very skilled professionals who can replace, rather than lose, the missing jobs (Haipeter, 2020).

Further and beyond these trade-offs, there is a growing concern that technological innovations do not fully benefit the industry in the Global South because ICT's functionality depends on internet connectivity. Some Global South countries lack the infrastructure to offer reliable broadband internet coverage that delivers quality high-speed internet. This significant technological limitation limits the possibility of achieving a better quality of life to about 3.6 billion people who remain offline (ITU News, 2020). Today more than ever, critical infrastructure and home-based jobs depend on high-speed internet access to the extent that it has become fundamental to exercise human rights (IACHR, 2020).

Wired technology is becoming obsolete, and indeed the next generations will not know about it unless they visit a science museum. Today, it is the use of wireless technology in its fourth generation, better known as 4G. Just as 4G technology displaced its previous generations, 2G and 3G, 5G technology has replaced 4G. In summary, 5G is the state-of-the-art network technology to support a large amount of data traffic; moreover, 5G promise to be a critical technology in the lead of the transition to a more sustainable future (Yu, Lee, & Jeon, 2017). According to Zikria, Kim, Afzal, Wang, and Rehmani (2018), 5G services can be categorised based on end users' experience as follow:

- Immersive 5G services – In this category are users that demand massive content streaming, virtual, augmented reality, and telepresence.

- Intelligent 5G services – This category encompasses crowded area service, user-centric computing, and Edge/Fog Computing.

- Omnipresent 5G services – This category encompasses users in several sectors such as intelligent personal devices, smart health building, intelligent grid city, and intelligent factory systems.

- Autonomous 5G services – The services in this category are demanding by smart transportation, teleoperation drone-based 3D connectivity, robot-based service.

- Public 5G services – This mode of service addresses users in resilient infrastructures such as private security and public safety disaster monitoring emergency service.

As tempting as this technological advance is to consolidate a more sustainable industry, its launch worldwide has been controversial. In recent years, a rumour about health hazards from 5G technology has captured the attention of many people on Twitter. A study found that the rumour was fed by an account that spread this conspiracy theory; although this account was closed by Twitter, some users genuinely took this rumour as accurate (Ahmed, Vidal-Alaball, Downing, & Lopez-Seguí, 2020). 5G conspiracy theories were not exclusive in Twitter; they also circulated widely in the community of Facebook (Bruns, Harrington, & Hurcombe, 2020). Incredible though it may seem, nonconformity spilled out of the cyber world into the real world. Massive protests broke out, mainly in the United Kingdom, where angry crowds attacked 5G antennas. A few decades ago, the debate about the harm to human health that electromagnetic waves could cause was in full swing, but one could take for granted that this debate was currently in disuse. This situation is not the case to the surprise of many, and today it has evolved to include 5G technology (Meese, Frith, &

Wilken, 2020). Whatever happens in the future, 5G technology will likely continue to be at the core of sustainability innovation. It is here where financial services are necessary to enable the industry to acquire the assets related to innovation. Thus, the following section of this chapter presents the importance of financial services as a fundamental component to achieve SDG9.

1.4. INCLUSIVE AND SUSTAINABLE INDUSTRIALISATION AND FINANCIAL SERVICES

Last but not least, this chapter is closed with a brief reflection on two critical concepts to understand what SDG9 all is about. The first concept is inclusive and sustainable industrialisation, which addresses all three dimensions of sustainable development: social equity, economic growth, and environmental protection (UNIDO, 2014). This concept is considered in target 9.2, which, to the letter, says as follows:

> *TARGET 9.2: Promote inclusive and sustainable industrialization and, by 2030, significantly raise industry's share of employment and gross domestic product, in line with national circumstances, and double its share in least developed countries. (U.N. General Assembly, 2017)*

The inclusive and sustainable industrialisation concept encourages an industry that does not generate pollution, protects workers' health, and, at the same time, is profitable. The idea goes further when trying to ensure that the benefits and contributions made by the industry to the country serve to improve the quality of life of those most in need. Indeed, employment generation in rural areas and the Global South remains the most significant challenge. According to a considerable body of business literature, helping the broader society should be included among the responsibilities and priorities of Chief Executive Officers (CEOs) and the board of directors (Denoncourt, 2020), but to what extent should industrial businesses be accountable for the people left behind? This question is never answered. Principles of legitimacy theory dictate that companies are immersed within society; they are not isolated; hence firms need to implement initiatives that favour society in exchange for community acceptance (Seguí-Mas, Polo-Garrido, & Bollas-Araya, 2018).

Commonly we tend to think that industries should carry a degree of social responsibility because it is the right thing to do. Still, if we reflect on this reasoning, we conclude that it is not enough from a business perspective. Firms' engagement in CSR strategies depends to a large extent on factors related to the CEOs, including level, gender, tenure, age, and compensation (Saridakis, Angelidou, & Woodside, 2020). The support of the CEO is important, but it is not the only requirement; it is also necessary to assess the administrative and financial particularities of the firm, as well as the current market conditions. Firms establish CSR strategies for many reasons, but at least they seek to legitimise their industrial activity and, if possible, better position themselves in the market (Sardana, Gupta, Kumar, & Terziovski, 2020). The companies that exercise substantive actions in favour of society go much further than greenwashing their image and establish an entire financial and logistical structure to fulfil their social commitment (Dahlin, Ekman, Röndell, & Pesämaa, 2020).

Although it might seem the opposite, medium and small companies are of great importance for countries in both developed and emerging economies to achieve SDG9; however, the potential to benefit society is limited due to their inadequate technical capacity and weak financial structure (van der Ven, 2018). Given this need, governments should facilitate granting credits to SMEs in the different industrial sectors and create fiscal stimuli that allow sustainable economic growth. For the same reason, target 9.3 refers to:

> *TARGET 9.3: Increase the access of small-scale industrial and other enterprises, in particular in developing countries, to financial services, including affordable credit, and their integration into value chains and markets. (U.N. General Assembly, 2017).*

The economic power of the financial services sector undoubtedly allows it to influence global policies on critical sustainability topics such as the energy sector or the transport sector (Carnicer & Peñuelas, 2012). However, SMEs are hard of interest to them. SMEs depend on loans from governments, banks, or private institutions in obtaining financial resources to keep operating. In this framework, the Microfinance institutions (MFIs) figure represents an affordable alternative for financing profitable and financially sustainable SMEs. However, they can hardly access loans from banking institutions (Githaiga, 2021). Currently, MFIs adapt to new market circumstances while meeting their initial core social objective; therefore, there is a risk that this source of financing undergoes adverse changes for access to funds (Navin & Sinha, 2021).

Last year, the world economy suffered one of its worst slowdowns, characterised by high unemployment rates, layoffs, and business closures everywhere. Undoubtedly, financing for sustainable development was affected in all sectors; therefore, innovative strategies are necessarily required to reactivate financial support. The 2020 Financing for Sustainability Report issued by Inter-agency U.N. Task Force on Financing for Development informs how the global economy is far from expected due to early pandemic disruptions. Furthermore, the report shows the count of the damages and the path towards financing for sustainability reactivation. The main findings in the report are highlighted below, which can be downloaded from the Department of Economic and Social Affairs website (United Nations, 2020).

In the report is claimed that the current unfavourable context is exacerbated by:

- Slowing economic growth;
- Declining assistance;
- Growing financial risks;
- High debt risk;
- Increasing trade restrictions; and,
- Increasing Environmental Shocks.

On the other hand, the report urges the following actions to better transit to the new normal

- Policies oriented to maintain economic and financial stability
- Promote trade and stimulate growth
- Increase donations to Official Development Assistance, mainly in the Least Development Countries (LDCs) and other low-income countries (LIC)
- Suspend debt payments to LDCs and other LICs
- Increase financial instruments to reduce climate risks and raise resources for SDG investments.

As we have learned throughout this chapter, SDG9 comprises important concepts intertwined with the fundamental idea of achieving an inclusive and sustainable industry where its benefits extend to less developed countries. Below is a summary of all of the above.

1.5. WRAP UP

First of all, we debated that stakeholders enabling resilient infrastructure must endorse sustainability principles to be better positioned to respond satisfactorily to high-risk weather events, that is, without serious incidents or fatalities. Developments in resilient infrastructure are driven by innovation, which has become of national importance because many countries base their economic growth on their national innovation capacity. Promoting sustainable industrialisation is not possible without technological innovation; in this context, the flourishing of industry 4.0 has based its development upon ICTs such as CPS, the Internet of Things (IoT), and Big Manufacturing Data Analytics. On the other hand, the adoption and proliferation of ICTs demand internet connectivity with much data traffic. This condition challenging to satisfy for a considerable percentage of the world population, especially for people in countries lacking advanced technology. Promote inclusive and sustainable industrialisation will not be possible if the industry does not have the means to acquire ICT. For this, cash flow must be restored as soon as possible to finance projects that promote environmental sustainability and social sustainability that allow the most vulnerable people in industrial development. Fig. 1.1 shows a graphical abstract of the chapter's content.

REFERENCES

Afzal, M., Lawrey, R., & Gope, J. (2019). Understanding national innovation system (NIS) using porter's diamond model (PDM) of competitiveness in ASEAN-05. *Competitiveness Review*, *29*(4), 336–355. doi:10.1108/CR-12-2017-0088

Ahmed, W., Vidal-Alaball, J., Downing, J., & Lopez-Seguí, F. (2020). COVID-19 and the 5G conspiracy theory: Social network analysis of Twitter data. *Journal of Medical Internet Research*, *22*(5), 1–9. doi:10.2196/19458

FUNDAMENTAL CONCEPTS OF SDG 9

Resilient Infrastructure

It is the system's capacity to return to its original state previous to a natural disaster as soon as possible

Innovation

Innovation relates to new products, services, processes, procedures, and ideas to foster Inclusive and Sustainable Industrialization

Information and Communication Technology

It is the adoption of the advancement of Industry 4.0 technologies such as Cyber-Physical Systems (CPS), Internet of Things (IoT), and Big Manufacturing Data Analytics

Inclusive and Sustainable Industrialization

The inclusive and sustainable industrialization concept encourages an industry that does not generate pollution, protects workers' health, and, at the same time, is profitable. The idea goes further when trying to ensure that the benefits and contributions made by the industry to the country serve to improve the quality of life of those most vulnerable.

Financial Services

This concept refers to the development of economic instruments that prioritize sustainability business models.

Fig. 1.1.   Fundamental Concepts of SDG9.

Amaral, A., & Peças, P. (2021). SMEs and Industry 4.0: Two case studies of digitalization for a smoother integration. *Computer in Industry*, *125*.

Angelopoulou, A., Mykoniatis, K., & Boyapati, N. R. (2020). Industry 4.0: The use of simulation for human reliability assessment. *Procedia Manufacturing*, *42*, 296–301.

Angulo, S., & Barrera, A. (2021). Texas freezes hits northern Mexico with $2.7 billion blackouts. *Reuters*. Retrieved from https://www.reuters.com/article/us-mexico-energy-idUSKBN2AG2HC. Accessed on May 10, 2021.

Baker, N. B., Khater, M., & Haddad, C. (2019). Political stability and the contribution of private investment commitments in infrastructure to GDP: An institutional perspective. *Public Performance and Management Review*, *42*(4), 808–835. doi:10.1080/15309576.2018.1523064

Bendix, T. (2021). Late Night Blasts Conservatives Blaming Windmills for Texas. *The New York Times*. February 18, p. N.A. (L). Gale Academic OneFile. Retrieved from link.gale.com/apps/doc/A652090604/AONE?u=purchase&sid=AONE&xid=63dc0906. Accessed on May 7, 2021.

Benitez, E. O., Becker da Costa, M., Baierle, I. C., Schaefer, J. L., Benitez, G. B., Aguiar Lima do Santos, L. M., & Benitez, L. B. (2021). Expected impact of industry 4.0 technologies on sustainable development: A study in the context of Brazil's plastic industry. *Sustainable Production and Consumption*, *25*, 102–122.

Bhupendra, K. V., & Sangle, S. (2015). What drives successful implementation of pollution prevention and cleaner technology strategy? The role of innovative capability. *Journal of Environmental Management*, *155*, 184–192. doi:10.1016/j.jenvman.2015.03.032

Biggi, G., & Giuliani, E. (2021). The noxious consequences of innovation: What do we know? *Industry and Innovation*, *28*(1), 19–41. doi:10.1080/13662716.2020.1726729

Binz, C., & Truffer, B. (2017). Global innovation systems: A conceptual framework for innovation dynamics in transnational contexts. *Research Policy*, *46*(7), 1284–1298. doi:10.1016/j.respol.2017.05.012

Blunt, K., & Passy, C. (2021). In Texas, Winter Storm Forces Rolling Power Outages as Millions Are Without Electricity; more than 150 million residents countrywide are under various weather warnings and advisories. *Wall Street Journal (Online)*, 1–4. Retrieved from https://ezproxy.purchase.edu/login?qurl=https%3A%2F%2Fwww.proquest.com%2Fn%0Aewspapers%2Ftexas-winter-storm-forces-rolling-power%02outages%2Fdocview%2F2489510549%2Fse-2%3Faccountid%3D14171%0D. Accessed on May 10, 2021.

Bruns, A., Harrington, S., & Hurcombe, E. (2020). 'Corona? 5G? or both?': the dynamics of COVID-19/5G conspiracy theories on Facebook. *Media International Australia*, *177*(1), 12–29. doi:10.1177/1329878X20946113

Calabrese, A., Castaldi, C., Forte, G., & Levialdi, N. G. (2018). Sustainability-oriented service innovation: An emerging research field. *Journal of Cleaner Production*, *193*, 533–548. doi:10.1016/j.jclepro.2018.05.073

Carnicer, J., & Peñuelas, J. (2012). The world at a crossroads: Financial scenarios for sustainability. *Energy Policy*, *48*, 611–617. doi:10.1016/j.enpol.2012.05.065

Carroll, J., Blas, J., & Dlouhy, J. (2021). Texas' Gas-Export Clampdown Shocks Market as Blackouts Ebb. *Bloomberg*. Retrieved from https://www.bloomberg.com/news/

articles/2021-02-17/texas-bans-natural-gas-companies-from-taking-fuel-out-of-state. Accessed on May 10, 2021.

Chang, S. E., Mcdaniels, T., Fox, J., Dhariwal, R., & Longstaff, H. (2014). Toward disaster-resilient cities: Characterizing resilience of infrastructure systems with expert judgments. *Risk Analysis*, *34*(3), 416–434. doi:10.1111/risa.12133

Chatterjee, A., & Layton, A. (2020). Mimicking nature for resilient resource and infrastructure network design. *Reliability Engineering and System Safety*, *204*. doi:10.1016/j.ress.2020.107142

Chirisa, I., Bandauko, E., Mazhindu, E., Kwangwama, N. A., & Chikowore, G. (2016). Building resilient infrastructure in the face of climate change in African cities: Scope, potentiality, and challenges. *Development Southern Africa*, *33*(1), 113–127. doi:10.1080/0376835X.2015.1113122

CNN. (2021). *Why snow and blackouts in Texas are a preview for all of us*. Retrieved from https://edition.cnn.com/videos/weather/2021/02/17/texas-blackout-climate-change-orig-jk.cnn/video/playlists/wicket-weather/. Accessed on May 11, 2021.

Dahlin, P., Ekman, P., Röndell, J., & Pesämaa, O. (2020). Exploring the business logic behind CSR certifications. *Journal of Business Research*, *112*(January), 521–530. doi:10.1016/j.jbusres.2019.11.046

Denoncourt, J. (2020). Companies and U.N. 2030 Sustainable Development Goal 9 industry, innovation and infrastructure. *Journal of Corporate Law Studies*, *20*(1), 199–235. doi:10.108 0/14735970.2019.1652027

Ehrenfeld, J. R. (2000). Industrial ecology paradigm shift or normal science? *American Behavioral Scientist*, *44*(2), 229–224. doi:10.1177%2F0002764200044002006

Englund, W. (2021). The fight over who will pay for Texas blackouts gears up. *Washington Post*, April 14, p. N.A. Gale Academic OneFile. Retrieved from link.gale.com/apps/doc/A658321365/AONE?u=purchase&sid=AONE&xid=7513 3e62. Accessed on May 7, 2021.

Enkel, E., & Gassmann, O. (2010). Creative imitation: Exploring the case of. *R&D Management*, *40*(3), 256–270. doi:10.1111/j.1467-9310.2010.00591.x

EOD Resilience Resources. (2016). *Introducing infrastructure resilience* (Issue July). Retrieved from http://dx.doi.org/10.12774/eod_tg.july2016.gallegolopezessex1. Accessed on August 15, 2021.

European Commission. (2020). *Responsible research & Innovation, Horizon*. Retrieved from https://ec.europa.eu/programmes/horizon2020/en/h2020-section/responsible-research-innovation. Accessed on May 19, 2021.

Fanning, R., Ament, J., & Brisbin, S. (2021). Across Texas, extreme cold brings rolling blackouts, traffic accidents and business closures. *Houston Public Media, a Service of the University of Houston*. Retrieved from https://www.houstonpublicmedia.org/articles/news/weather/2021/02/15/391490/across-texas-extreme-cold-brings-rolling-blackouts-traffic-accidents-and-business-closures/. Accessed on May 11, 2021.

Firozi, P. (2021). Texas officials launch investigation into enormous power bills after last week's storm. *Washington Post*, February 21, p. N.A. Gale Academic OneFile. Retrieved from link.gale.com/apps/doc/A652579556/AONE?u=purchase&sid=AONE&xid=5356310c. Accessed on May 7, 2021.

Freeman, J. (2017). The uncomfortable convergence of energy and environmental law. *Environmental & Energy*

Law Program, 1–84. Retrieved from https://eelp.law.harvard.edu/2017/08/freeman-on-the-uncomfortable-convergence-of-energy-and-environmental-law/. Accessed on August 14, 2021.

Ghobakhloo, M. (2018). The future of manufacturing industry: A strategic roadmap toward Industry 4.0. *Journal of Manufacturing Technology Management*, 29(6), 910–936. doi:10.1108/JMTM-02-2018-0057

Githaiga, P. N. (2021). Revenue diversification and financial sustainability of microfinance institutions. *Asian Journal of Accounting Research*, ahead-of-print. doi:10.1108/ajar-11-2020-0122

Golz, S. (2016). Resilience in the built environment: How to evaluate the impacts of flood resilient building technologies? *FLOODrisk 2016- 3rd European Conference on Flood Risk Management*, 7, 1–13. doi:10.1051/e3sconf/20160713001

Gromek, P., & Sobolewski, G. (2020). Risk-based approach for informing sustainable infrastructure resilience enhancement and potential resilience implication in terms of emergency service perspective. *Sustainability (Switzerland)*, 12(11). doi:10.3390/su12114530

Haipeter, T. (2020). Digitalisation, unions and participation: The German case of 'industry 4.0'. *Industrial Relations Journal*, 51, 242–260. doi:10.1111/irj.12291

Helmrich, A. M., Chester, M. V., Hayes, S., Markolf, S. A., Desha, C., & Grimm, N. B. (2020). Using biomimicry to support resilient infrastructure design. *Earth's Future*, 8(12). doi:10.1029/2020EF001653

Hetemi, E., Ordieres-Meré, J., & Nuur. (2020). An institutional approach to digitalization in sustainability-oriented infrastructure projects: The limits of the building information model. *Sustain*. 12, 3893. doi:10.3390/su12093893

Hilty, L. M., Arnfalk, P., Erdmann, L., Goodman, J., Lehmann, M., & Wäger, P. A. (2006). The relevance of information and communication technologies for environmental sustainability: A prospective simulation study. *Environmental Modelling and Software*, *21*(11), 1618–1629. doi:10.1016/j.envsoft.2006.05.007

Hostettler, S. (2018). From innovation to social impact. In S. Hostettler, S. Besson, & J.-C. Bolay (Eds.), *Technologies for development* (pp. 3–9). Cham: Springer. doi:10.1007/978-3-319-91068-0_2

Huck, A., Monstadt, J., Driessen, P. P. J., & Rudolph-Cleff, A. (2021). Towards Resilient Rotterdam? Key conditions for a networked approach to managing urban infrastructure risks. *Journal of Contingencies and Crisis Management*, *29*(1), 12–22. doi:10.1111/1468-5973.12295

IACHR. (2020). *How to promote universal internet access during the COVID-19 pandemic?* (pp. 1–10). Retrieved from https://www.oas.org/es/cidh/sacroi_covid19/documentos/03_guias_practicas_internet_ing.pdf. Accessed on April 25, 2021.

ITU & UN-OHRLLS. (2018). *Achieving universal and affordable Internet in the least developed countries*. Retrieved from http://unohrlls.org/custom-content/uploads/2018/01/D-LDC-ICTLDC-2018-PDF-E.pdf. Accessed on May 25, 2021.

ITU News. (2020). *Tech v COVID-19: Managing the crisis*, *3*. Retrieved from https://www.itu.int/en/itunews/Documents/2020/2020-03/2020_ITUNews03-en.pdf. Accessed on April 25, 2021.

Jackson, S. A., Gopalakrishna-Remani, V., Mishra, R., & Napier, R. (2016). Examining the impact of design for environment and the mediating effect of quality management innovation on firm performance. *International Journal of Production Economics*, *173*, 142–152. doi:10.1016/j.ijpe.2015.12.009

Jarmai, K. (2020). Learning from sustainability-oriented innovation. In K. Jarmai (Ed.), *Responsible innovation business opportunities and strategies for implementation*. Dordrecht: Springer. http://www.springer.com/series/13811

Kayal, A. A. (2008). National innovation systems a proposed framework for developing countries. *International Journal of Entrepreneurship and Innovation Management*, 8(1), 74–86. doi:10.1504/IJEIM.2008.018615

Kennedy, C., & Corfee-morlot, J. (2013). Past performance and future needs for low carbon climate resilient infrastructure – An investment perspective. *Energy Policy*, 59, 773–783. doi:10.1016/j.enpol.2013.04.031

Kirchherr, J., & Urban, F. (2018). Technology transfer and cooperation for low carbon energy technology: Analysing 30 years of scholarship and proposing a research agenda. *Energy Policy*, 119, 600–609. doi:10.1016/ j.enpol.2018.05.001

Lanfranchi, M. (2010). Sustainable technology as an instrument of the environmental policy for the attainment of a level of socially acceptable pollution. *Word Futures*, 66(6), 449–454. doi:10.1080/02604020903423543

Lasi, H., Fettke, P., Feld, T., & Hoffmann, M. (2014). Industry 4.0. Business & Information Systems Engineering. doi:10.1007/s12599-014-0334-4

Lim, S. S., & Sonko, L. K. (2019). Linking corporate sustainability and innovation in supply chain management: Evidence of a Taiwan leading glass recycling company. *Technology Analysis and Strategic Management*, 31(8), 957–971. doi:10.1080/09537325.2019.1575957

MacArthur, J. L., Hoicka, C. E., Castleden, H., Das, R., & Lieu, J. (2020). Canada's Green New Deal: Forging the socio-political foundations of climate resilient infrastructure? *Energy Research and Social Science*, *65*(February), 101442. doi:10.1016/j.erss.2020.101442

Meese, J., Frith, J., & Wilken, R. (2020). COVID-19, 5G conspiracies and infrastructural futures. *Media International Australia*, *177*(1), 30–46. doi:10.1177/1329878X20952165

Melvin, J. (2021). Texas blackouts may bring FERC winterization mandates, shape federal spending. *SNL Energy Power Daily; Charlottesville*, 1–3. Retrieved from https://ezproxy.purchase.edu/login?qurl=https%3A%2F%2Fwww.proquest.com%2Ftr. Accessed on May 7, 2021.

Musiolik, J., Markard, J., & Hekkert, M. (2012). Networks and network resources in technological innovation systems: Towards a conceptual framework for system building. *Technological Forecasting and Social Change*, *79*(6), 1032–1048. doi:10.1016/j.techfore.2012.01.003

Naser, M. Z. (2019). Autonomous and resilient infrastructure with cognitive and self-deployable load-bearing structural components. *Automation in Construction*, *99*, 59–67. doi:10.1016/j.autcon.2018.11.032

Navin, N., & Sinha, P. (2021). Social and financial performance of MFIs: Complementary or compromise? *Vilakshan – XIMB Journal of Management*, *18*(1), 42–61. doi:10.1108/xjm-08-2020-0075

Niu, B., Shanshan, E., Cao, Y., Xiao, J., Zhan, L., & Xu, Z. (2021). Utilizing E-waste for construction of magnetic and core-shell Z-scheme photocatalysts: An effective approach to E-waste recycling. *Environmental Science and Technology*, *55*, 1279–1289. doi:10.1021/acs.est.0c07266

Ottoni, M., Dias, P., & Xavier, L. H. (2020) A circular approach to the e-waste valorization through urban mining in Rio de

Janeiro, Brazil. *Journal of Cleaner Production*, *261*, 120990. https://www.x-mol.com/paperRedirect/1237092406113583104

Pashkevich, N., Haftor, D., Karlsson, M., & Chowdhury, S. (2019). Sustainability through the digitalization of industrial machines: Complementary factors of fuel consumption and productivity for forklifts with sensors. *Sustainability*, *11*, 1–21. doi:10.3390/su11236708

Patil, R. A., & Ramakrishna, S. (2020). A comprehensive analysis of e-waste legislation worldwide. *Environmental Science and Pollution Research*, *27*, 14412–14431. doi:10.1007/s11356-020-07992-1

Pedro, F., Giglio, E., Velazquez, L. V., & Munguia, N. (2021). Constructed governance as solution to conflicts in e-waste recycling networks. *Sustainability*, *13*, 1–22. doi:10.3390/su13041701

Perera, A. T. D., Javanroodi, K., & Vahid, M. N. (2021). Climate resilient interconnected infrastructure: Co-optimization of energy systems and urban morphology. *Applied Energy*, *285*(August 2020), 116430. doi:10.1016/j.apenergy.2020.116430

Practical Engineering. (2021). *What really happened during the Texas power grid outage?* https://practical.engineering/blog/2021/3/22/what-really-happened-during-the-texas-power-grid-outage. Accessed on August 14, 2021.

Romeo, J. (2010). Banking on Green. *Cadalyst*, *Fall*, 14–17. Retrieved from https://www.cadalyst.com/collaboration/product-lifecycle-management/banking-green-13627. Accessed on May 22, 2021.

Sardana, D., Gupta, N., Kumar, V., & Terziovski, M. (2020). CSR 'sustainability' practices and firm performance in an emerging economy. *Journal of Cleaner Production*, *258*, 1–10. doi:10.1016/j.jclepro.2020.120766

Saridakis, C., Angelidou, S., & Woodside, A. G. (2020). What type of CSR engagement suits my firm best? Evidence from an abductively-derived typology. *Journal of Business Research*, *108*, 174–187. doi:10.1016/j.jbusres.2019.11.032

Schwartz, M., Peglow, F., Fritsch, M., & Günther, J. (2012). What drives innovation output from subsidized R&D cooperation? – Project-level evidence from Germany. *Technovation*, *32*(6), 358–369. doi:10.1016/j.technovation.2012.03.004

Seguí-Mas, E., Polo-Garrido, F., & Bollas-Araya, H. M. (2018). Sustainability assurance in socially sensitive sectors: A worldwide analysis of the financial services industry. *Sustainability 10*(8), 1–21. doi:10.3390/su10082777

Smith, A. (2021). Here's why gas and coal went offline during the Texas cold weather catastrophe. *Washington Examiner*. Retrieved from https://www.washingtonexaminer.com/policy/gas-coal-offline-texas-cold-snap. Accessed on May 11, 2021.

Spencer, J. H., & Meng, B. (2019). Resilient urbanization and infrastructure governance: The case of the Phnom Penh Water Supply Authority, 1993–2007. *Water Policy*, *21*(4), 848–864. doi:10.2166/wp.2019.211

Stakheyeva, H. (2018). Intellectual property and competition law: Understanding the interplay. In A. Bharadwaj, I. Gupta, & V. H. Devaiah (Eds.), *Multi-dimensional approaches towards new technology: Insights on innovation, patents and competition*. Singapore: Springer. doi:10.1007/978-981-13-1232-8

Szopik-Depczyńska, K., Kędzierska-Szczepaniak, A., Szczepaniak, K., Cheba, K., Gajda, W., & Ioppolo, G. (2018). Innovation in sustainable development: An investigation of the E.U. context using 2030 agenda indicators. *Land Use Policy*, *79*(July), 251–262. doi:10.1016/j.landusepol.2018.08.004

The World Bank. (2020). *Private Participation in Infrastructure (PPI)*. Retrieved from file:///C:/Users/52662/Downloads/PPI_2020_Half-Year_Update.pdf. Accessed on May 06, 2021.

Tilley, D. R. (2003). Industrial ecology and ecological engineering: Opportunities for symbiosis. *Journal of Industrial Ecology*, 7(2), 13–32. doi:10.1162/108819803322564325

U.N. General Assembly. (2017). *Global indicator framework for the Sustainable Development Goals and targets of the 2030 Agenda for Sustainable Development*, July 6, A/RES/71/313. Retrieved from https://unstats.un.org/sdgs/indicators/indicators-list/. Accessed on March 22, 2021.

UNIDO. (2014). *Inclusive and sustainable industrial development: Creating shared prosperity, safeguarding the environment*. Retrieved from https://www.unido.org/sites/default/files/files/2019-06/DG_Brochure_February_2015_Web.pdf. Accessed on May 15, 2021.

United Nations. (2020). Inter-agency Task Force on Financing for Development, Financing for Sustainable Development Report 2020. New York. Retrieved from https://developmentfinance.un.org/fsdr2020. Accessed on May 29, 2021.

van der Ven, C. M. A. (2018). Inclusive industrialization: The interplay between investment incentives and SME Promotion Policies in Sub-Saharan Africa. *Law and Development Review*, 11(2), 557–587. doi:10.1515/ldr-2018-0029

Veer, T., & Jell, F. (2012). Contributing to markets for technology? A comparison of patent filing motives of individual inventors, small companies and universities. *Technovation*, 32(9–10), 513–522. doi:10.1016/j.technovation.2012.03.002

Velazquez, L., Bello, D., Munguia, N., Zavala, A., Marin, A., & Moure-Eraso, R. (2008). A survey of environmental and occupational work practices in the automotive refinishing industry of a developing country: Sonora, Mexico. *International Journal of Occupational and Environmental Health*, *14*(2), 104–111. doi:10.1179/oeh.2008.14.2.104

Wang, Q., Kong, L., Li, J., Li, B., & Wang, F. (2020) Behavioral evolutionary analysis between the government and uncertified recycler in China's E-waste recycling management. *Int. J. Environ. Res. Public Health*, *17*, 1–15.

Wang, L., & Xu, X. (2019). Sustainable cybernetic manufacturing. *International Journal of Production Research*, *57*(12), 3799–3801. doi:10.1080/00207543.2019.1598153 EDITORIAL

Wiesmeth, H. (2020). Stakeholder engagement for environmental innovations. *Journal of Business Research*, *119*(March 2018), 310–320. doi:10.1016/j.jbusres. 2018.12.054

Yu, H., Lee, H., & Jeon, H. (2017). What is 5G? Emerging 5G mobile services and network requirements. *Sustainability (Switzerland)*, *9*(10), 1–22. doi:10.3390/su9101848

Zhang, W. (2019). Constitutional Governance in India and China and its impact on national innovation. In K.-C. Liu & U. S. Racherla (Eds.), *Innovation, economic development, and intellectual property in India and China*. Singapore: Springer. doi:10.1007/978-981-13-8102-7_20

Zhang, W., Zheng, Q., Ashour, A., & Han, B. (2020). Self-healing cement concrete composites for resilient infrastructures: A review. *Composites Part B: Engineering*, *189*(February), 107892. doi:10.1016/j.compositesb.2020.107892

Zikria, Y. B., Kim, S. W., Afzal, M. K., Wang, H., & Rehmani, M. H. (2018). 5G mobile services and scenarios: Challenges and solutions. *Sustainability (Switzerland)*, *10*(10), 1–9. doi:10.3390/su10103626

2

SUSTAINABILITY REPORTING ON SDGS

ABSTRACT

To perform a detailed analysis of the inherent complexities in achieving the 9th Sustainable Development Goal (SDG), it is necessary to understand the procedures used by member states delegations to follow-up and review the progress made in implementing the SDGs and targets as mandated in the A/RES/70/1 Resolution adopted by the General Assembly on September 25, 2015 (U.N. General Assembly, 2015); best known worldwide as 'Transforming our world: the 2030 Agenda for Sustainable Development'. Hence, this chapter aims at providing an overview of sustainability reporting practices to the U.N. High-level Political Forum on Sustainable Development (HLPF). It starts by reflecting on the U.N. landmark events from which the 2030 Agenda emerged and the political and cultural context prevailing at that time. Afterward, it argues on the guidance documents issued by HLPF for following up and reviewing individual countries' progress. The most controversial issue covered in this chapter undoubtedly concerns information gathering. This issue is because stakeholders consistently question the accuracy of data being provided, not only on Voluntary National Reviews (VNRs) but also on corporate sustainability reports. Therefore, the chapter also covers the guidelines of independent external organisations such as the Global Compact Initiative (GCI) and Global Reporting Initiative (GRI) used by firms to legitimate sustainability reporting content and increase reliability. Finally, this chapter concludes with a brief description of required procedures to submit and present VNRs.

Keywords: High-level Political Forum on Sustainable Development; Voluntary Common Reporting Guidelines; *Handbook for the Preparation of VNR*; global indicator framework; Voluntary National Reviews; Global Compact Initiative; Global Reporting Initiative

1.1. LANDMARK U.N. EVENTS

Visioning sustainable industrialisation had been a recurrent ambition since almost 30 years ago. The background to the Agenda 2030 is a series of U.N. world summits, which started with the Rio Earth Summit in 1992. In the first action plan of the U.N. concerning sustainable development, Agenda 21, many issues were focussing on unsustainable patterns of production and consumption that call for minimising the depletion of natural resources and the reduction of pollution (United Nations Conference on Environment and Development & Sitarz, 1993).

In 2000, the eight Millennium Development Goals (MDGs) were aimed to eliminate the gravest problems confronted in human life, mainly those regarding the African continent. The eight goals were eradicating extreme poverty and hunger, accomplishing universal primary education, promoting gender inequity and woman autonomy, reducing child mortality, improving maternal health, fighting HIV/AIDS and other diseases, guaranteeing environmental sustainability, and promoting global partnerships. Although the term industry was barely mentioned in the resolution, stopping unsustainable production and consumption patterns was intrinsically connected to the MDGs (U.N. General Assembly, 2000).

Tenaciously, the U.N. encouraged industry during the World Summit on Sustainable Development 2002 to develop models for promoting sustainability when engaging in responsible business practice (United Nations, 2003). Twenty years after the Earth Summit, the World Summit on Sustainable Development 2012 was held by U.N. again in Brazil to define 'the future, we want'. On this document, the U.N. called upon industry to take into account the importance of corporate social responsibility by enhancing collaboration with governmental entities and other stakeholders to implement sustainability initiatives (United Nations, 2012).

The era of MDGs ended in 2015, emphasising the importance of integrating environmental concerns into global value chains in electronics, automotive, garments, and service industries (UN-MDG Gap Task Force, 2015). Those developments have led us to the 2030 Agenda, conceived as the MDGs' continuation, but with a new deadline to meet the targets and goals. The latest U.N. Agenda aims to meet 17 SDGs by 2030 (U.N. General Assembly, 2015). Still, without overlooking the interconnection among the 17 SDGs, only a few are applicable in industrial settings (Huatuco & Ball, 2019). SDG9 is the most significant for all industry sectors because it seeks new inclusive and sustainable industrialisation avenues. The following section explores some guidance documents to understand the process and procedure to report on SDG9.

1.2. U.N. GUIDANCE DOCUMENTS

The U.N. High-level Political Forum on Sustainable Development (HLPF) is at the core of the United Nations platform for follow-up and reviewing the countries' progress towards the

2030 Agenda. This Forum is positioned in the U.N. system under the Economic and Social Council (ECOSOC), and its format and organisational aspects are found in the resolution A/RES/67/290 (U.N. General Assembly, 2013). Furthermore, according to the eighty-second paragraph of the resolution A/RES/70/1 (U.N. General Assembly, 2015), the main tasks of the HLPF are:

a) To facilitate the sharing of experiences, successes, challenges, and lessons learned.

b) To provide political leadership, guidance, and recommendation for follow-up.

c) To promote system-wide coherence and coordination of sustainable development policies.

d) To ensure that the 2030 Agenda remains relevant, ambitious and focuses on assessing progress, achievements, and challenges faced by countries and new and emerging issues.

e) To establish effective linkages with the follow-up and review of all relevant U.N. Conferences and Processes, including least developed countries, small island developing States, and landlocked developing countries.

In addition, the generation of information and data processing procedures is significant to elaborate VNRs. Consequently, the 2030 agenda address this issue in its seventy-ninth paragraph, which states:

> *[...] Member States to conduct regular and inclusive reviews of progress at the national and sub-national levels, which are country-led and country-driven. Such reviews should draw on contributions from indigenous peoples, civil society, the private sector, and other stakeholders, in line with national circumstances, policies, and priorities.*

> *National parliaments, as well as other institutions, can also support these processes. (A/RES/70/1, p. 33)*

Voluntary National Reviews (VNRs) are the cornerstone instrument by which member state delegations report to the U.N. HLPF their 2030 Agenda's achievements. When preparing their VNR, members' states must observe 11 principles described in paragraph 74 of the 2030 Agenda; of them all, particular attention should be paid to the first principle, which states that:

> *The follow-up and review processes will be voluntary and country-led, will take into account different national realities, capacities, and levels of development, and will respect policy space and priorities. As national ownership is key to achieving sustainable development, the outcome from national-level processes will be the foundation for reviews at the regional and global levels, given that the global review will be primarily based on national official data sources.*

Three U.N. guidance documents underpin the process to conduct and deliver VNR as dictated by the 2030 Agenda. The first guidance document is the Voluntary Common Reporting Guidelines for VNRs. These guidelines offer support to member states by defining the sections and content on VNRs. The most recent update was made in January 2021 (U.N. Committee for Development Policy, 2021), showing the guiding principles and the structure and content of a report for the HLPF. In this report, it is essential to highlight the progress on sustainable development goals (SDGs) and their targets. It is also demanded to explain the means of implementation. Finally, a presentation is required at the HLPF.

To articulate the Voluntary Common Reporting Guidelines, the HLPF has published a handbook, the second guidance document, to enable member states to elaborate a VNR (UN

DESA, 2021). In addition, this handbook indicates procedures to organise and prepare a review about build back better. It also asks to include the participation of all stakeholders. Finally, the guide requests to submit and present the VNR at the HLPF.

To operationalise and complement both the standard reporting guidelines and the *Handbook for the Preparation of VNR*, the U.N. General Assembly adopted in 2017, Resolution A/RES/71/313, the global indicator framework (GIF) to guide governments in their SDG reporting (U.N. General Assembly, 2017). This framework was developed by the Inter-Agency and Expert Group on SDG indicators. It refers to 231 official indicators plus their targets to outline countries' voluntary reviews. In addition, it recommends collecting disaggregated data by income, sex, age, race, ethnicity, migratory status, disability, geographic location, or other characteristics. Finally, the framework is regularly evaluated and, if necessary, adapted to the current world's necessities. Concerning SDG9, the framework offers the targets previously mentioned in chapter one.

Now that we understand the requirements to elaborate a VNR, it is time to learn how the information is gathered. This process is more complicated than earlier because it depends on several external factors that are difficult for the National Statistical Offices to control.

1.3. INFORMATION GATHERING

As previously noted, countries need to access reliable data to inform their achievements to the HLPF. Questions are raised on how voluntary corporate sustainability reports are considered in VNRs; regrettably, there is no straightforward answer to this enigma. Undoubtedly, it requires a close partnership among governments, industrial sub-sectors, and diverse stakeholders; otherwise, many SDG initiatives would be entirely unreported. In general, governments rely on National Statistical Offices to produce quality data in their national statistical systems. Most member states gather data through regulatory reporting mandated in federal environmental legislation. Over the years, governments have been acclaimed to be one of the more robust drivers to encourage corporate sustainability through legislation or supporting voluntary reporting (Adaui, 2020). International treaties and agreements have catalysed the convergence of sustainability regulatory requirements among nations (Fernandez, 2018), causing many national environmental regulations worldwide to be stricter over time (Holzinger, Knill, & Sommerer, 2011). Several factors may influence the stringency of different countries' environmental reporting policies, including the economic situation, social values, and cultural factors (Martínez-Ferrero & García-Sánchez, 2017).

As mentioned in the guidance documents and in the 2030 Agenda itself, VNRs should consider the inputs from many stakeholders such as civil society, the private sector, trade unions, members of parliament, and national human rights institutions. Regardless of whether sustainability reporting must be, or not, imposed, at present, the issue of sustainability reports is becoming increasingly common among firms to meet stakeholders' growing demands and expectations; yet, concerns are raised about the lack of standardisation in the content of what is reported, the lack of quantitative performance indicators, and consequently, the considerable subjectivity involved in the firm's reports (Delbard, 2008; Siew, 2015; Stewart & Niero, 2018). This situation creates mistrust and suspicion among relevant stakeholders about the integrity of the information disclosure. Hence, the need to provide reasonable levels of assurance over the accuracy of the information on voluntary sustainability reports confirming their reliability.

For the sake of transparency, objectivity, and creditability, hiring the services of an independent external organisation seems to be the most widely adopted strategy to legitimate the sustainability reporting content (Jones, Hillier, & Comfort, 2016). The decision to hire an independent assurance company should have evidence of a positive cost-benefit ratio. According to Ruhnke and Gabriel (2013), the business's size is one of the most critical determinant factors when hiring an external assuring company; consequently, large firms' administrative and financial structures are better positioned to surpass the service's cost. Other essential factors in purchasing assurance are the relation between the cost of providing responsible activities compared to the benefits obtained, the quality of the assurance, and the pressure of responding to external demands (Bagnoli & Watts, 2017).

After gathering all information, the member states must submit and present their VNRs to the HLPF. The following section briefly describes this process.

1.4. VNR SUBMISSION AND PRESENTATION

After gathering information and preparing the VNR document, member states must submit it to the HLPF and prepare themselves to present it. Items F and G in the *Handbook for the Preparation of VNR* offer guidelines to conduct these procedure phases. During the preparation process, the U.N. Department of Economic and Social Affairs (UN DESA) organises a series of workshops based on countries' previous experiences in participating in the VNR process. The member states' representatives participate by sharing experiences to facilitate peer learning.

The submission phase is finalised by delivering two documents to the U.N. Department of Economic and Social Affairs, the Secretariat of the HLPF. The first document contains the Main Messages for their VNRs, and the Second contains the final VNR report. Once VNRs are received, the HLPF conducts follow-up work to assess the nation's progress towards the 2030 Agenda and the SDGs. Additionally, member states are requested to submit audio-visual materials highlighting the implementation of the 2030 Agenda in their countries to support their VNR presentation.

The presentation should convey the key findings of the VNRs, including good practices, challenges, and areas for support and advice. Once all countries in the session have presented, questions are posed to the presenting countries. In accordance with past practice, countries presenting a VNR for the first time will have 15 minutes for their presentation, followed by a similar amount of time for questions from other countries and stakeholders and factoring in time for podium changes. The 15-minute time allocation includes the use of audio-visual material, including videos.

According to the Resolution A/RES/70/299,

> *the sequence of themes for each four-year cycle of the forum shall reflect the integrated, indivisible and interlinked nature of the Sustainable Development Goals and the three dimensions of sustainable development, including cross-cutting issues as well as new and emerging issues, and will serve as the framework for reviewing all 17 Goals. (U.N. General Assembly, 2016)*

The theme of the meeting of the HLPF in 2017 was eradicating poverty and promoting prosperity in a changing world, which included the analysis of the Sustainable Development Goal 9 Industry, Innovation, and Infrastructure. The following HLPF in 2021 will cover the theme Sustainable and resilient recovery from the COVID-19 pandemic that promotes the economic, social, and environmental dimensions of sustainable development: building an inclusive and effective path for the achievement of the 2030 Agenda in the context of the decade of action and delivery for sustainable development. At this meeting, 10 countries will present their first VNR, 25 countries will offer their VNR for the second time, and 9 for the third time (UN DESA, 2020).

Although they are not obliged to contract an external audit, it is common for governments to hire an external audit service to ensure that the information contained in their report includes what is required in the guidance documents. The following section deals with this external assurance process.

1.5. EXTERNAL ASSURANCE FRAMEWORKS

External assurance aims to ensure that content in a sustainability report is relevant and credible (Akisik & Gal, 2020). Currently, there are in the market several external frameworks to ensure the quality of sustainability reports. Two of the most prestigious and controversial frameworks are presented below.

1.5.1. The United Nations Global Compact

Within all sustainability assurance frameworks, the United Nations Global Compact is one of the most important, if not the most. In 2000, the U.N. Global Compact was created to engage private firms to collaborate with United Nations to foster corporate practices that protect human and labour rights, the environment and fight to eradicate corruption (U.N. Global Compact, 2014). Business involvement on the Global Compact is based on incorporating 10 principles into its strategic planning.

The first two principles, related to Human Rights and derived from the Universal Declaration of Human Rights, state:

> *Principle 1: 'Businesses should support and respect the protection of internationally proclaimed human rights; and'*

> *Principle 2: 'Make sure that they are not complicit in human rights abuses'.*

Concerning labour and derived from the International Labor Organization's Declaration on Fundamental Principles and Rights at Work, the following four principles establish that:

> *Principle 3: 'Businesses should uphold the freedom of association and the effective recognition of the right to collective bargaining'.*

> *Principle 4: 'The elimination of all forms of forced and compulsory labor'.*

> *Principle 5: 'The effective abolition of child labor; and'*

> *Principle 6: 'The elimination of discrimination in respect of employment and occupation'.*

Related to the environment and derived from the Rio Declaration on Environment and Development, the following three principles are aimed at enhancing corporate sustainability:

> *Principle 7: 'Businesses should support a precautionary approach to environmental challenges'.*

> *Principle 8: 'Undertake initiative to promote greater environmental responsibility'.*

> *Principle 9: 'Encourage the development and diffusion of environmentally friendly technologies'.*

Related to Anti-corruption practices and derived from the U.N. Convention Against Corruption principle 10 advises:

> *Principle 10: 'Businesses should work against corruption in all its forms, including extortion and bribery'.*

In its 2020-year progress report, U.N. Secretary-General asserted that:

> *Over its 20-year history, the Compact has guided companies of all sizes and from all regions to embed*

a principles-based approach to doing business. It has also brought the voice of responsible business into global agenda-setting discussions, including on the Sustainable Development Goals and Paris Agreement on Climate Change. (U.N. Global Compact, 2020)

In terms of affiliates, the Global Compact has succeeded in increased the number of companies and reports. As of April 2021, the Global Compact's website includes more than 13,043 companies from 160 countries and hosts 79,597 public reports (U.N. Global Compact, 2021b). These stats are updated periodically.

We should be cautiously optimistic about these impressive results and not raise expectations very high. In the past, detractors have sharply criticised the Global Compact for having no performance requirements (Nason, 2008). It has also been said that the Global Compact allows businesses to claim success to boost their corporate image, but without showing objective evidence (Voegtlin & Pless, 2014). Furthermore, uncertainties in the evidence displayed on annual reporting instruments called Communication on Progress (COP) led to minimal accountability for company members (Williams, 2014). In a recent study, Jastram and Klingenberg (2018) confirm that the U.N Global Compact is intensely used in strategic management, but objectives are not evaluated in many organisations. Besides, the lack of more stringent requirements to prove progress has raised concerns about companies trying to take advantage of participating in the Global Compact Initiative (GCI) but continuing to do business as usual (Rasche, Waddock, & McIntosh, 2012). This practice is known as 'Bluewashing', which refers to companies that collaborate with any U.N. Agency and declare to be compliant with the ten principles while not. After reflecting on these, and other critiques, Sethi and Schepers (2014) concluded that the loss of public trust from some constituencies, the viability, usefulness, and existence of GCI were uncertain. In the same sense,

Berliner and Prakash (2015) agree about the risk of losing credibility at the global level if companies keep practicing shirking.

A prestigious executive Director of the U.N. Global Compact confronted criticism towards GCI, arguing that the success of the Global Compact is based on the continued relevance of the initiative's underlying idea, the sustained institutional leadership support, the governmental support (political back-up), and the operational viability of the initiative rather than other criteria (Kell, 2013). At present, the U.N. Global Compact consolidates a new strategy to strengthen the way businesses will fulfil the principles mentioned above while meeting the SDGs (U.N. Global Compact, 2021a). This strategy recognises that it is necessary to consider that the COVID-19 pandemic has severely disrupted most of the firms' efforts to meet all SDGs; consequently, the world is behind in achieving the 2030 Agenda, as it was planned.

1.5.2. The Global Reporting Initiative

Another tool for voluntary sustainability reporting is the Global Reporting Initiative (GRI), an independent non-governmental organisation based in Amsterdam, which comprises voluntary initiatives from companies worldwide. The GRI applies to any organisation regardless of its size, type, sector, or geographic location. In its 2020a, GRI Sustainability Reporting Standards document (p. 3, 2020), the GRI claims that:

> *Sustainability reporting based on the GRI Standards should provide a balanced and reasonable representation of an organization's positive and negative contributions towards the goal of sustainable development.*

According to the GRI document, the GRI offers the following two sets of Sustainability Reporting Standards: Universal and Topic-Specific Standards. The universal standards provide general guidelines to elaborate the report. The topic-specific standards are grouped according to the three dimensions of sustainable development. For example, the first group of them is labelled as GRI 200. This group comprises seven standards aimed at the economic dimension of sustainability. The GRI 300 group includes eight standards that address topics related to the environmental dimension of sustainability. Finally, the third group, GRI 400, contains 19 GRIs that focus on the social dimension of sustainable development.

The GRI standards are based on ten principles specified in GRI 101; the first four principles define report content and the following six principles for determining report quality. The first group involves the following principles: Stakeholder Inclusiveness, Sustainability Context, Materiality, and Completeness. Then, the GRI standards are complemented by Accuracy, Balance, Clarity, Comparability, Reliability, and Timeliness principles. Last updated by December 2020, its sustainability disclosure database contains over 38,481 GRI reports; 63,849 reports from about 15,431 organisations (GRI, 2020b).

The latter results are not without their critics. Even though the GRI's success in the increased dissemination and standardisation of sustainability reporting is recognised; still, those who now criticise the GRI state that this achievement does not guarantee the effectiveness of assurance related to improving accountability and transparency (Junior & Best, 2017). The lack of determination of materiality in the GRI reports has often become a matter of significant disagreement among those who criticised the GRI reports' shortcomings. Barkemeyer, Preuss, and Lee (2015) analysed 933 GRI reports by companies from 30 countries and found that most of the reports have not met the principle of materiality. Only about 4 out of 10 reports disclose environmental performance information. Some go as far as suggesting that the lack of Materiality on GRI reports could have the hidden purpose of avoiding sustainability performance disclosures (Slacik & Greiling, 2019). The picture is worst in developing countries where the GRI has limited impact on increasing sustainability reports (Tauringana, 2020). The lack of economic and financial resources and inadequate institutional support are the most significant constraints preventing adopting the GRI framework in developing countries (Tilt, Qian, Kuruppu, & Dissanayake, 2020).

As we have learned in this chapter, preparing, submitting, and presenting the progress report of the 2030 Agenda is challenging, to put it in a friendly way. For this reason, there is a critical thought that doubts the legitimacy of sustainability reports, which is evident in the scientific literature.

1.6. WRAP UP

This chapter has addressed the complexities of sustainability reporting to meet the Sustainability Developments Goals by 2030. To recapitulate, VNRs are the cornerstone instrument by which a member state delegations report to the U.N. HLPF their 2030 Agenda's achievements.

The Voluntary Common Reporting Guidelines for VNRs, the *Handbook for the Preparation of VNR*, and the GIF are U.N. guidance documents to guide member states' delegation to SDG reporting. External assurance is essential to meet critical stakeholders' demands. In this context, the U.N. Global Compact and the GRI are the most prestigious and controversial frameworks. Fig. 2.1 shows a graphical abstract of the chapter's content.

REFERENCES

Adaui, C. R. L. (2020). Sustainability reporting quality of Peruvian listed companies and the impact of regulatory requirements of sustainability disclosures. *Sustainability (Switzerland)*, 12(3), 1–22. doi:10.3390/su12031135

NON-LINEAR ROADMAP TO SUSTAINABILITY REPORTING ON SDGS

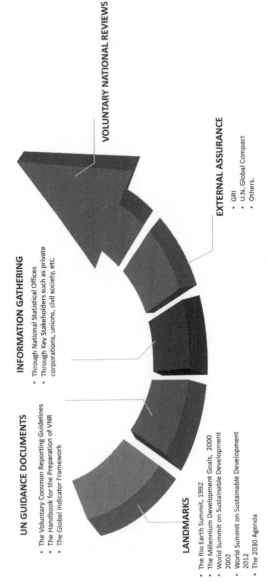

Fig. 2.1. Non-Linear Roadmap to Sustainability Reporting on SDGs.

Akisik, O., & Gal, G. (2020). Integrated reports, external assurance, and financial performance: An empirical analysis on North American firms. *Sustainability Accounting, Management and Policy Journal, 11*(2), 317–350. doi:10.1108/SAMPJ-02-2019-0072

Bagnoli, M., & Watts, S. G. (2017). Voluntary assurance of voluntary CSR disclosure. *Journal of Economics and Management Strategy, 26*(1), 205–230. doi:10.1111/jems.12171

Barkemeyer, R., Preuss, L., & Lee, L. (2015). On the effectiveness of private transnational governance regimes-Evaluating corporate sustainability reporting according to the Global Reporting Initiative. *Journal of World Business, 50*(2), 312–325. doi:10.1016/j.jwb.2014.10.008

Berliner, D., & Prakash, A. (2015). "Bluewashing" the firm? Voluntary regulations, program design, and member compliance with the United Nations global Compact. *Policy Studies Journal, 43*(1), 115–138. doi:10.1111/psj.12085

Delbard, O. (2008). CSR legislation in France and the European regulatory paradox: An analysis of EU CSR policy and sustainability reporting practice. *Corporate Governance, 8*(4), 397–405. doi:10.1108/14720700810899149

Fernandez, R. M. (2018). Interactions of regional and national environmental policies: The case of Spain. *Cogent Economics and Finance, 6*(1), 1–16. doi:10.1080/23322039.2018.1442092

Global Reporting Initiative (GRI). (2020a). *Consolidated set of GRI Sustainability Reporting Standards 2020*. Retrieved from https://www.globalreporting.org/how-to-use-the-gri-standards/gri-standards-english-language/. Accessed on April 15, 2021.

Global Reporting Initiative (GRI). (2020b). *Sustainability Disclosure Database*. Retrieved from http://datebase.globalreporting.org. Accessed on April 20, 2021.

Holzinger, K., Knill, C., & Sommerer, T. (2011). Is there convergence of national environmental policies? An analysis of policy outputs in 24 OECD countries. *Environmental Politics*, *20*(1), 20–41. doi:10.1080/09644016.2011.538163

Huatuco, L. H., & Ball, P. D. (2019). The quest for achieving United Nations sustainability development goals (SDGs) production and consumption. *RAUSP Management Journal*, *54*(3), 357–362. doi:10.1108/RAUSP-04-2019-0068

Jastram, S. M., & Klingenberg, J. (2018). Assessing the outcome effectiveness of multi-stakeholder initiatives in the field of corporate social responsibility – The example of the United Nations Global Compact. *Journal of Cleaner Production*, *189*, 775–784. doi:10.1016/j.jclepro.2018.04.005

Jones, P., Hillier, D., & Comfort, D. (2016). Materiality and external assurance in corporate sustainability reporting: An exploratory study of Europe's leading commercial property companies. *Journal of European Real Estate Research*, *9*(2), 147–170. doi:10.1108/JERER-07-2015-0027

Junior, M. R., & Best, P. (2017). GRI G4 content index: Does it improve credibility and change the expectation–performance gap of GRI-assured sustainability reports? *Sustainability Accounting, Management and Policy Journal*, *8*(5), 571–594. doi:10.1108/SAMPJ-12-2015-0115

Kell, G. (2013). 12 years later: Reflections on the growth of the U.N. global compact. *Business and Society*, *52*(1), 31–52. doi:10.1177/0007650312460466

Martínez-Ferrero, J., & García-Sánchez, I. M. (2017). Coercive, normative and mimetic isomorphism as determinants of the voluntary assurance of sustainability reports. *International Business Review*, *26*(1), 102–118. doi:10.1016/j.ibusrev.2016.05.009

Nason, R. W. (2008). Structuring the global marketplace: The impact of the United Nations global compact. *Journal of Macromarketing*, *28*(4), 418–425. doi:10.1177/0276146708325388

Rasche, A., Waddock, S., & McIntosh, M. (2012). The United Nations global compact: Retrospect and prospect. *Business and Society*, *52*(1), 6–30. doi:10.1177/0007650312459999

Ruhnke, K., & Gabriel, A. (2013). Determinants of voluntary assurance on sustainability reports: An empirical analysis. *Journal of Business Economics*, *83*(9), 1063–1091. doi:10.1007/s11573-013-0686-0

Sethi, S. P., & Schepers, D. H. (2014). United Nations global compact: The promise-performance gap. *Journal of Business Ethics*, *122*(2), 193–208. doi:10.1007/s10551-013-1629-y

Siew, R. Y. J. (2015). A review of corporate sustainability reporting tools (SRTs). *Journal of Environmental Management*, *164*, 180–195. doi:10.1016/j.jenvman.2015.09.010

Slacik, J., & Greiling, D. (2019). Compliance with Materiality in G4-sustainability reports by electric utilities. *International Journal of Energy Sector Management*, *14*(3), 583–608. doi:10.1108/IJESM-03-2019-0010

Stewart, R., & Niero, M. (2018). Circular economy in corporate sustainability strategies: A review of corporate sustainability reports in the fast-moving consumer goods sector. *Business Strategy and the Environment*, *27*(7), 1005–1022. doi:10.1002/bse.2048

Tauringana, V. (2020). Sustainability reporting challenges in developing countries: Towards management perceptions research evidence-based practices. *Journal of Accounting in Emerging Economies*, *11*(2), 194–215. doi:10.1108/JAEE-01-2020-0007

Tilt, C. A., Qian, W., Kuruppu, S., & Dissanayake, D. (2020).
The state of business sustainability reporting in sub-Saharan
Africa: An agenda for policy and practice. *Sustainability
Accounting, Management and Policy Journal*, 12(2), 267–296.
doi:10.1108/SAMPJ-06-2019-0248

U.N. Committee for Development Policy. (2021). The 2020
VNRs: points for reflection in preparation for the 2021
reviews *(Issue April)*. Retrieved from https://www.un.org/
development/desa/dpad/wp-content/uploads/sites/45/CDP-
Reflections-2021-VNRs.pdf. Accessed on May 18, 2021.

U.N. Department of Economic and Social Affairs (UN DESA).
(2020). *First Global Webinar for the Voluntary National
Reviews to be presented at the U.N. high-Level Political
Forum on Sustainable Development in 2021*. Retrieved from
https://www.un.org/en/desa/welcome-remarks-first-global-
webinar-2021-hlpf-vnrs. Accessed on April 15, 2021.

U.N. Department of Economic and Social Affairs (UN DESA).
(2021). *Handbook for the preparation of voluntary national
reviews*. Retrieved from https://sustainabledevelopment.un.org/
content/documents/27024Handbook_2021_EN.pdf. Accessed
on March 25, 2021.

U.N. General Assembly. (2000). *United Nations Millennium
Declaration, Resolution Adopted by the General Assembly*,
September 18, A/RES/55/2. Retrieved from https://www.refworld.
org/docid/3b00f4ea3.html. Accessed on March 24, 2021.

U.N. General Assembly. (2013). *Format and Organizational
aspects of the high-level political Forum on sustainable
development*. Retrieved from https://undocs.org/
pdf?symbol=en/a/res/67/290. Accessed on April 15, 2021.

U.N. General Assembly. (2015). *Transforming our world: The
2030 Agenda for Sustainable Development*, October 21,

A/RES/70/1. Retrieved from https://www.refworld.org/docid/57b6e3e44.html. Accessed on March 24, 2021.

U.N. General Assembly. (2016). *Fellow-up and review of the 2030 Agenda for Sustainable Development at the global level*. Retrieved from https://www.cbd.int/doc/meetings/mar/soiom-2016-01/other/soiom-2016-01-desa-unga-a-70a_res_70_299-en.pdf

U.N. General Assembly. (2017). *Global indicator framework for the Sustainable Development Goals and targets of the 2030 Agenda for Sustainable Development*, July 6, A/RES/71/313. Retrieved from https://unstats.un.org/sdgs/indicators/indicators-list/. Accessed on March 22, 2021.

U.N. Global Compact. (2014). *Guide to corporate sustainability – Shaping a sustainable future*. Retrieved from https://d306pr3pise04h.cloudfront.net/docs/publications%2FUN_Global_Compact_Guide_to_Corporate_Sustainability.pdf. Accessed on March 28, 2021.

U.N. Global Compact. (2020). *Uniting business in the decade of action: Building on 20 Years of Progress*. Retrieved from https://globalcompact.no/wp-content/uploads/2020/06/publikasjon.pdf. Accessed on March 25, 2021.

U.N. Global Compact. (2021a). *Revision to the U.N. Global Compact's Reporting Framework- The communication on Progress (CoP)*. Retrieved from https://ungc-communications-assets.s3.amazonaws.com/docs/publications/UNGC_CoP_Revision_Info_Note.pdf. Accessed on March 25, 2021.

U.N. Global Compact. (2021b) *Affiliates statistics*. Retrieved from https://www.unglobalcompact.org. Accessed on April 20, 2021.

UN-MDG Gap Task Force. (2015). *Taking stock of the global partnership for development*. New York. Retrieved from https://www.un.org/millenniumgoals/pdf/MDG_Gap_2015_E_web.pdf. Accessed on March 22, 2021.

United Nations. (2003). *Johannesburg Declaration on Sustainable Development and Plan of Implementation of the World Summit on Sustainable Development: The final text of agreements negotiated by governments at the World Summit on Sustainable Development*, 26 August–4 September 2002, Johannesburg, South Africa. New York, NY: United Nations Department of Public Information. Retrieved from https://digitallibrary.un.org/record/499757. Accessed on March 22, 2021.

United Nations. (2012). *Report of the United Nations conference on sustainable development*. Rio de Janeiro, Brazil. Retrieved from https://undocs.org/en/A/CONF.216/16. Accessed on March 22, 2021.

United Nations Conference on Environment and Development, & Sitarz, D. (1993). *AGENDA 21: The Earth Summit strategy to save our planet*. Boulder, CO: EarthPress.

Voegtlin, C., & Pless, N. M. (2014). Global Governance: CSR and the Role of the U.N. Global Compact. *Journal of Business Ethics*, *122*(2), 179–191. doi:10.1007/s10551-014-2214-8

Williams, O. F. (2014). The United Nations global compact: What did it promise? *Journal of Business Ethics*, *122*(2), 241–251. doi:10.1007/s10551-014-2219-3

3

ASSESSING PROGRESS TOWARDS
THE ACHIEVEMENT OF SDG9

ABSTRACT

The U.N.'s perseverance in fostering sustainable industrialisation has not rendered the expected results in the long run. Despite that the scope of SDG9 is reasonably well defined and communicated, there is much more to be done to make it a reality. Achievements on SDG9 have not been as positive as they might have. It should be noted that there is no trustworthy source of information that indicates with certainty the progress towards the 2030 agenda. The purpose of this chapter is to examine factors involved in the SDG9 reporting and other critical issues necessary to understand the progress and how we are progressing towards SDG9. From this point on, data for our debate come from several sources. Still, the primary outcomes come from the 2017 High-level Political Forum on Sustainable Development, the Sustainable Development Goals Report 2020, the 2020 Voluntary National Reviews (VNRs) independent assessment, and other Sustainable Development Goals (SDGS) reports as well as scientific literature. Unfortunately, there appears to be a lack of reliable SDG9 information available, and what exists is hard to find. In general, information sources often offer qualitative information, and quantitative data are scarce. This situation is especially the case for the documents presented in the chapter, which provided a few statistics disaggregate data, making it challenging to analyse in-depth. The debate here presented does not seek to be a fully comprehensive assessment of their content. The analysis is not designed to interpret or replace the referenced documents, either. Instead, it is intended to illustrate the difficult task of measuring the progress towards SDG9.

Keywords: SDG9; sustainability reporting; sustainability indicators; VNR assessments; interconnectedness; National Statistical Systems

2.1. TRACKING PROGRESS

This section reports insights from three U.N. sources about the progress towards the 2030 agenda and other unofficial reports. We looked specifically for valuable data in text excerpts explicitly related to SDG9, but we tried to figure out insights from general outcomes or implicit evidence when it was not possible.

2.1.1. 2017 High-level Political Forum on Sustainable Development

The SDG9 was in-depth reviewed during the 2017 High-level Political Forum on Sustainable Development. Information on the Ministerial declaration of the 2017 high-level political forum on sustainable development can be found in the following reference (U.N. Economic and Social Council, 2017). Forty-three countries presented their Voluntary National Reviews under the theme 'Eradicating poverty and promoting prosperity in a changing world'. The Economic and Social Council president offered an optimistic factual summary about the implementation of the SDGs, yet countries were warned that many people were being left behind (HLPF, 2017). In addition, the president of the council provided industry insights from the expert panels. The main ideas are recapitalised below:

a) It was reiterated that the manufacturing industry continues to underpin economic growth.

b) The manufacturing industry was essential to keep the economic development, employment, and social stability.

c) Development countries would need support from development partners in improving infrastructure and connectivity to foster their industrialisation.

d) Similarly, governments should help small and medium-sized enterprises (SMEs) and micro-enterprises by offering fiscal stimulus and effective policy to foster innovation.

e) Industrialisation growth must not harm the environment.

f) The promotion of resilient and green infrastructure should prioritise the safety of citizens and provide solutions for both mitigation and adaptation to climate change.

Another document generated during the 2017 HLPF was the Business & Industry Major Group Position Paper (Business and Industry Major Group, 2017). The content on this manuscript recognised the following critical issues to meet the SDG9:

1. The importance of investing in resilient infrastructure for delivering reliable energy, clean water, communications, logistics, and mobility.

2. The importance of improved collaboration among private and public sector actors.

3. The importance of fostering innovation and scientific and technological advancement.

4. The importance of partnership with governments and other stakeholders.

5. The importance of encouraging capacity building and education initiatives.

6. The importance of investing in connectivity infrastructure, next-generation broadband technologies, high-speed networks, and Information and Communication Technologies.

7. The importance of developing reliable and predictable transit infrastructure and services that would facilitate trade.

In closing, the 2017 HLPF issued one document with two ministerial declarations, the Ministerial Declaration of the high-level segment of the 2017 session of the Economic and Social Council on the annual theme 'Eradicating poverty in all its forms and dimensions through promoting sustainable development, expanding opportunities, and addressing related challenges' and the Ministerial declaration of the 2017 high-level political forum on sustainable development, convened under the auspices of the Economic and Social Council, on the theme 'Eradicanting poverty and promiting prosperity in a changing world'.

A summary of SDG9's conclusions is offered in the 18th paragraph of the document. It emphasises the importance of resilient infrastructure, innovation, and industry to meet the common goal of achieving inclusive and sustainable economic development to eradicate poverty. It recognised the role of sustainable industrialisation in transforming economies to create essential factors such as creating decent jobs, productivity growth, energy efficiency, innovation, and social inclusion. Reflecting on these conclusions, it was reasonable to categorise it as an appropriate kickoff to start monitoring SDG9, but a more significant disruption was still to come. Nobody could then seriously foresee that by 2020 this optimism would be modified by the COVID-19 pandemic. Since then, the pandemic treated and changed the lives of millions of human beings worldwide. The subsequent report to be presented in this chapter is the SDGs 2020 report. Data in the report were gathered before the pandemic; still, the report presents the initial impacts of COVID-19. While the counting of affectation continues, the SDGs 2020 report provides an initial assessment carried out by the U.N. Department of Economic and Social Affairs.

2.1.2. The 2020 SDGs Report

This section analyses critical aspects included in the Sustainable Development Goals Report 2020, which can be download from the U.N. Department of Economic and Social Affairs website (United Nations, 2020). According to the report itself, the document was prepared by the United Nations Department of Economic and Social Affairs in collaboration with over 200 experts from more than 40 international agencies using the latest available data and estimates. Although our main interest is to analyse SDG9, it is also essential to debate general provisions included in the report.

In its foreword, the Secretary-General of the United Nations recognised three critical issues about the SDGs:

1. SDGs require immense political will and ambitious action by all stakeholders.

2. Progress remains uneven, and we were not on track to meet the SDGs by 2030.

3. The COVID-19 pandemic is making the achievement of SDGs even more challenging.

For its part, the Under-Secretary-General for Economic and Social Affairs reiterated that the disruptions caused by the pandemic effect and turned back in some SDGs, the progress towards the 2030 Agenda for Sustainable Development, highlighting the greater vulnerability of the world's poorest people. But, on the other hand, it also encourages governments and businesses to build a healthier, more resilient, and more sustainable world. None of the above statements were unknown; however, the issues take another dimension when the United Nations' highest authorities claim those because member state delegation and other key stakeholders cannot ignore this call for action.

While recognising the limitation of huge data gaps among countries, the report's results inform that the proportion of countries reporting data on SDG9 is one of the highest among all SDGs. Nearly 80 countries report meeting SDG9 just below SDG3, SDG5, and SDG15. Moreover, the SDGs data timeliness is average from 2017, which is acceptable considering that just six of the SDGs report under more recent data. The SDG9 infographic provides data about the air transport industry, manufacturing growth, financing for small-scale industries, investment and research and development, and internet connectivity. The SDG9 infographic is complemented with briefs but valuable insights, which are summarised below:

a) The air transport industry has been profoundly affected by the COVID-19 pandemic, and it is predicted huge industry losses before recovery from the crisis.

b) Lockdowns shut off most manufacturing operations in many businesses everywhere, causing unprecedented disruptions to global supply chains.

c) Small and medium-sized manufacturers are struggling to get finance to produce their goods. Therefore, the report clarifies the need to facilitate access to financial services and fiscal stimulus to strengthen and maximise their competitiveness, whether in national or international markets.

d) The report paid a great deal of attention to the importance of increasing Research and Development investment, mainly in the pharmaceutical industry and emerging technologies. For example, COVID-19 has forced the pharmaceutical industry to increase its R&D investment budgets to create, as soon as possible, vaccines, diagnostic tests, and treatments for SARS-CoV-2.

e) The reports pointed out that the pandemic exacerbated the digital divide, mainly in the least developed countries. When internet connectivity is essential to work, study, and socialise from home, about half of the world's population cannot access the Internet and other basic communication services because it is unaffordable for them or they do not have the required knowledge.

According to the updated data, the SDGs 2020 report leaves no doubt that meeting the SDGs by 2030 has become more and more unlikely. More alarming, the poorest are not covering their basic needs despite the motto 'Leaving No One Behind', which best sums up the guiding principles and compromises on the 2030 Agenda. Moreover, the COVID-19 pandemic seriously exacerbated conditions in almost all sectors and reversed progress towards all SDGs, especially those related to SDG9. Unfortunately, the lack of sufficiently disaggregated statistical data explored so far in U.N. documents does not allow us to understand fully all intricacies and details involved in SDG9. To address these shortcomings, independent assessments of SDG9 and scientific literature are added to this analysis.

2.1.3. VNR Assessments

As mentioned in the introduction of this chapter, looking in detail at the set of VNRs or a particular VNR is beyond the scope of this chapter. It would be simply unfeasible and impractical to try it. So instead, we are going to learn insights from three external assessments. The first document to analyse is a

U.N. information brief based on the 2020 VNR conducted by the Committee for Development Policy (CDP) (UN Committee for Development Policy, 2021). This committee is a subsidiary body of the Economic and Social Council that has analysed the voluntary national reviews annually since 2017 and advises the Council on various development issues. One of the points for consideration by the governments and other stakeholders participating in the 2021 VNRs suggests that the most commonly unreported goals in the 2020 VNRs are those most closely related to the environment, sustainability and climate change, and inequality. This suggestion might indirectly concern those industries and businesses prioritising SDG9, although this assumption is not expressly mentioned in the document. SDG9 is not listed among the least attention SDGs or targets in the 2020 VNRs.

A novel independent VNR assessment gives us a second clue. The authors present the key messages arising from the analysis of 2020 VNR reports (De Oliveira & Kindornay, 2021). In the content, the author claims the following:

This review of VNR reports is comprehensive and covers most, if not all, aspects of 2030 Agenda implementation and VNR reporting. As a result, the report has a lot to offer governments, civil society, researchers and others interested in understanding the current state of 2030 Agenda implementation and reporting, including good practices.

This report provides detailed descriptive information about general trends found in the 47 VNR reports submitted to the HLPF in 2020; however, regarding SDG9, the review offers just a few insights. Two of the most striking general findings are that when compared to previous VNRs, fewer countries showed baseline and gap assessments in their 2020 VNR, and fewer countries disclose information on data availability. In addition, the goal by goal analysis shows that 39 countries reported the

SDG9. Still, it does not provide further specific SDG9 information related to initiatives carried out by governments and their stakeholders. However, it is noted, '*a slight reverse in the positive trend in VNR reports towards greater detail in the examination of SDGs, targets, and indicators*'.

The fourth report of the local and regional governments (LRGs) to the HLPF: Towards the Localisation of the SDGs (UCLG, 2020) facilitated by the United Cities and Local Governments is our third source of information section. Sadly enough, LRGs do not pay enough attention to SDG9. Therefore, SDG9 is not expressly discussed throughout the report's content. On the other hand, some issues related to SDG9, such as urbanisation and resilient societies, are considered implicitly in the report, but it is hard to gain insights.

Built on the premise that the latest overview gives you a good picture of what is being reported, it can be inferred that SDG9 receives average attention from governments in the 2020 VNR. So, we need to continue digging into more sources of information.

2.1.4. SDG Good Practices Compilation UN DESA Report

This report was elaborated by The United Nations Department of Economic and Social Affairs (UN DESA, 2019). The information in the report does not come from VNR, and the legal disclaimer informs that the United Nations does not endorse the accuracy or reliability of any advice, opinion, statement, or outcomes provided by the stakeholders. This initiative tracked the good practices, success stories, and lessons learned in SDG implementation from governments, the United Nations system, civil society, the private sector, and other stakeholders worldwide from November 2018 to February 2019. SDG9 is one of the three SDGs with fewer governmental or community-based initiatives submitted in this compilation. According to the report's foreword, this collection was built upon a previous call launched by UN DESA in 2018. A team of experts scrutinised submissions from around 20 United Nations entities, and more than 500 selected initiatives were made available on an online platform. As demonstrative initiatives to inspire others, the document shows 16 SDG Good Practices representing 5 geographical regions. North America, Latin America, and The Caribbean have the largest share of initiatives considering the SDG9 fundamental, four out of four. The European and the ASIA-PACIFIC regions addressed SDG9 in one out of three initiatives. The African region presents four initiatives, but only in one is SDG9 addressed. Finally, Western ASIA offers no initiatives addressed to meet SDG9.

Considering the previous information in the last U.N. reports about the industry's significance to the Agenda 2030, this report's outcomes are a surprise. Still, at the same time, they encourage us to analyse some elements to understand the causes of the lower representation of this SDG in sustainability reporting (S.R.) means.

2.1.5. The 20th Anniversary of the United Nations Global Compact Report

This Global Compact report was issued, in collaboration with an independent provider of sustainability and risk management services, on the occasion of the twentieth anniversary of the United Nations Global Compact. As a reminder from the first chapter, the United Nations Global Compact is a corporate sustainability initiative launched in 2000 by the U.N. Secretary-General. The purpose of this report was to

> assess the progress made by the U.N. Global Compact business participants to date and looked ahead to what systemic changes are needed to reach the Sustainable Development Goals by 2030. (U.N. Global Compact, 2020)

This report shows an interesting study with a kind of scholarly methodology. Between February and May 2020, the research team gathered data from five sources of information: the U.N. Global Compact Annual Implementation Survey, structured Interviews, Case Studies, A sample of Communication on Progress disclosures, and Desktop research. The study's subject comprises sectors aligned with the Industry Classification Benchmark (ICB) taxonomy, which the U.N. Global Compact has used for all annual surveys. These systems are the following:

1. Energy, Natural Resources, and Basic Materials

2. Industrial Manufacturing

3. Food, Beverage, and Consumer Goods

4. Healthcare and Life Sciences

5. Mobility and Transportation

6. Telecommunications and Technology

7. Financial Services.

Findings related to SDG9 are more than acceptable, among which the following stand out:

1. Survey respondents recognised SDG9 as the second most relevant and significant, which indicates that SDG9 is one of the most embedded into their core business.

2. SDG9 is the most urgent priority for 59% of the Industrial manufacturing system.

3. SDG9 is a priority for 57% of the Telecommunications and Technology system and 53% of the Financial Services system.

4. SDG9 does not appear as one of the less prioritised goals in any of the seven systems.

5. SDG9 takes fourth place in the prioritising list. Again, 80%
   of companies prioritised Goal 9 to ensure all business infrastructure and capital projects by established criteria, and
   69% also extend their core expertise to improve national
   infrastructure.

As it can be observed, this report offers a good perspective of
the importance of SDG9 for business in the U.N. Global Compact. Perhaps the content in that report is not very accurate, but
it shows more or less the industry's positive contribution to the
SDGs. Beyond findings, the ICB used to determine the systems
allows us to figure out the nature of business prioritising SDG9.
So far, previous reports gave us the idea that inputs for SDG9
come from Industrial Manufacturing, Mobility and Transportation, and Telecommunications and Technology. Still, now we
gain more insight into SDG9 by understanding that inputs also
may come from Financial Services firms.

The outcomes in the report can be complemented with data
from the U.N. Global Compact website (U.N. Global compact,
2021b) that display a list of sectors that have reported activities to advance the SDG9. The most significant participation is
given in the following sectors: support services, construction and
materials, general industrials, financial services, software and
computer services, food producer, chemicals, electricity, electronic and electrical equipment, banks, diversified, industrial engineering, general retailers, industrial transportation, automobiles
and parts, gas–water-multiutilities, travel and leisure, technology
hardware and equipment, oil and gas producers, industrial metal
and mining, real-estate investment and services, media, mobile
telecommunications, pharmaceuticals and biotechnology, health
care equipment and services, personal goods, beverages, for-
estry and paper, fixed-line telecommunications, aerospace and
defense, alternative energy, oil equipment services and distribu-
tions, mining, household goods and home construction, nonlife

insurance, life insurance, leisure goods, food and drugs retailers, real-estate investment and trust, industrial goods and services, equity investment instruments, real-estate, nonequity investment instruments, primary resources, utilities, technology, retail, tobacco, oil and gas, health care, and finally, food and beverages. The website also ranks SDG9 in seventh place among the most relevant SDGs, with 13,500 companies reporting activities to advance SDG9.

2.1.6. The Sustainable Development 2020: Reporting the Impacts of COVID-19

Considering the magnitude of the COVID-19 pandemic worldwide, this document reports on COVID-19 disruptions to SDGs, emphasising the affectation of the pandemic on progress towards the entire set of SDGs (Sachs et al., 2020). Regarding SDG9, the report informs on mixed or moderately negative short-term impacts, which are summarised as follow:

- A decline in industrial outputs
- Possible nationalisation of some industries, and bankruptcies and closures of others
- Scientific collaboration to find treatments and vaccine
- Accelerated uptake of digital technologies for e-health, e-education, e-governance, and e-payments.

In the long term, the effects of the pandemic could be more serious, but it is still difficult to predict them accurately without falling into the realm of speculation. An insight that we have not noticed from previous reports is that SDG9 has been one of the three SDGs that show more progress or, in other words, one of the goals that are closer to be met. Then the document focus on reporting the SDG index profile by country. For this goal, authors gathered data primarily from international organisations such as the World Bank, the Organization for Economic Co-operation and Development (OECD), the World Health Organization (WHO), The FOOD and Agriculture Organization (FAO), The International Labour Organization (ILO), The U.N. International Children's Emergency Fund (UNICEF), and others. The OECD countries get the highest score in SDG9, and the lowest score is by Oceania. However, in the majority of countries' profiles, SDG9 shows a positive indicator. Last but not least, the report highlights the lack of reliable data and the urgent need to increase the statistical capacity of national statistical systems, which reiterates what has been discussed several times in this chapter.

Complementary information on SDG9 has been gathered from SDG reports, but they do not imply an assessment. However, they offer a little extra information to complete the final picture. These briefs are shown at the next incise.

2.1.7. Complementary Information Resources

Firstly, the World Business Council for Sustainable Development issued the Vision 2050 report with more than 40 global business leaders. For the first time in recent years, sustainability multistakeholders extent their deadline to reach sustainability from 2030 to 2050. In a certain way, the unfeasibility to meet the SDGs by 2030 is recognised. The Vision 2050 report is a framework for action in the decade ahead that is practical, grounded in reality, and designed to help companies drive change in their corporate sustainability. The report presents a figure with extrapolated data from UN DESA. In this figure, SDG9 is a little further than a moderate distance to meet the targets. This place is excellent considering that, except for SDG8, the other goals are behind it. The significance of SDG9 to the Vision 2030 is made manifest in the following pathways: energy, target 9.4;

transportation & mobility, target 9.1; living spaces, targets 9.1 & 9.4; products & materials, target 9.4; financial products & services, target 9.3; and connectivity, target 9.3 (WBCSD, 2021).

Additionally, the International Institution for Sustainable Development (IISD) maintains the 'SDG Knowledge Hub' project at its internet site. The project tracks SDG information and operates a web-based repository of information on SDGs rather than an assessment (IISD, 2021). The coverage of SDG9 includes 57 guest articles, 58 policy briefs, 6 generations 2030, 1,437 news, and 366 events. In total, SDG9 is the twelfth of the SDGs' coverage list, with 15% of all publications.

It can be concluded to close this section that SDG9 is, in most cases, unnoticed and almost invisible in many of SDG's reports and assessments. Despite its significance previously mentioned, SDG9 is given insufficient or very little attention in reporting on ensuring sustainable industrial development. This condition might stem from inadequate monitoring and lack of SDG9 data in countries across the Global South reporting 2020 VNRs. Now, we are turning the debate to another critical issue related to reporting, sustainability indicators. The following section briefly discusses the importance of selecting sustainability indicators for assessing progress to SDG9.

2.2. SUSTAINABILITY INDICATORS

As the years pass by, a substantial amount of sustainability indicators (S.I.s) appears to assess sustainability progress from governments, industries, and many other types of organisations. Some of the most widely used indicators in countries' sustainability reports are the Gross Domestic Product (GDP), the Index of Sustainable Economic Welfare (ISEW), and the Human Development Index (HDI); however, Kunčič (2018) warning us about the use of these indicators and the risk of making wrong conclusions at a subregional level that lead to missing out opportunities.

Moreover, sustainability indicators, such as the above, have always carried the stigmatisation of hiding valuable information for the sake of simplifying the decision-making process.

As a reminder, the global indicator framework (GIF) encompasses 231 official indicators plus their targets to outline countries' voluntary reviews. To be realistic, it is not feasible to meet all of them. It is, therefore, advisable to prioritise those goals and targets that align better with national strategies (Allen et al., 2017). Similarly, and in practical terms, the industry must recognise what SDGs relate more to their operations (Huatuco & Ball, 2019). In this case, expert judgement plays a central role in scrutinising VNRs and data interpretation in answering questions concerning targets and revealing if the content is addressed to conceal unfavourable data using rhetoric and official discourses (Lillehagen, Heggen, Tomson, & Engebretsen, 2020).

One might expect quantitative data in national voluntary reviews, but it is not the standard in most countries. Twenty-six countries' reports found that qualitative assessments prevailed over quantitative assessments (Allen, Metternicht, & Wiedmann, 2018). This reality has raised significant concerns, especially when measuring some immensurable socioecological properties of sustainability (Reid & Rout, 2020). Another matter is selecting sustainability indicators and the method applied to calculate them, which could significantly hamper an objective assessment (Allen, Reid, Thwaites, Glover, & Kestin, 2020). Currently, there is a growing requirement for metricised forms of governance, but those measurements often distort information for external accountability.

Moreover, as Bell and Morse (2018) concluded, sustainability indicators can be selectively used to support or discard any argument depending on the subjectivity and arbitrariness of the reporters' perspective. To this respect, some argue that firms should focus on their principal obligation to shareholders to generate utility, while others appeal to their corporate social responsibility (Scheyvens, Banks, & Hughes, 2016). In the case of SDG9, tools geospatial information systems have strengthened the capacity to generate quantitative data to assess the sustainability of a system, target 9.1.1, especially in developed countries (Ilie, Brovelli, & Coetzee, 2019).

The optimum selection of sustainability indicators should simplify data while maximising unique, relevant information (Garrett & Latawiec, 2015). For this reason, governments must evaluate the trade-offs between the benefits of agglutinate all complexities coexisting in a sustainable ecosystem in a single data, or a few data, and losing a big part of the picture. Furthermore, every effort has to be made to increase the credibility of the information reported. Therefore, the most accurate reporting must rely on the complementarity between quantitative and quantitative indicators.

This insight corroborates the U.N. warning, which fully recognised that the lack of reliable information represents one of the significant COVID-19 disruptions to regain the Agenda 2030 momentum before the pandemic. Consequently, it leaves us out of time to meet most SDGs (United Nations, 2020). Leaving no one behind implies recognising the interconnectedness among all SDGs. Unfortunately, there is a lack of indicator-based tools that integrate SDG implementation, and most assessments focus on a single SDG (Horan, 2020). In the next section, we discuss the complexity of this issue.

2.3. SDGS INDIVISIBILITY, INTEGRATION, AND INTERCONNECTEDNESS

SDGs' indivisibility, integration, and interconnectedness are widely recognised in almost all U.N. documents and published literature related to the 2030 Agenda. For example, practitioners and academics have stressed the interconnection between SDG9 with SDG12 to promote innovative and sustainable business models (Labbate et al., 2021). In addition, Sinha, Sengupta, and Alvarado (2020) suggest that policy level transformation would help nations advance towards reaching the SDG9, the SDG13, climate action, the SDG8, decent work and economic growth, the SDG7, clean and affordable energy, and SDG4, quality education, and SDG13.

Similarly, Rosado-González, Palacio-Prieto, and Abreu-Sá (2020) claim that the targets 9.2, 9.4, and 9.c exert significant influence on SDG8; and SDG10; SDG11, and SDG15. Recently, a research team evaluated the integrated nature of the SDG targets in the Arab region; the researchers found evidence to understand the strong interlinkage between target 9.4 sustainable infrastructure and environmentally sound technologies targeting 1.5 disaster resilience (Allen, Metternicht, & Wiedmann, 2019). Another study identified policy clusters formed by closely related SDGs; in the methodological design, goal nine was clustered with goals 1, 2, 6, 8, and 12 to foster resilient product systems (Obersteiner et al., 2016). For its part, Gromek and Sobolewski (2020) highlighted the interconnection among all targets in SDG9 with targets in SDG11 and SDG13. It makes sense because the only way to conceive sustainable cities is to be resilient to climate change. Hoek (2018), however, states arguments to link SDG9 with SDG6, clear water, and sanitation, and SDG3, Good Health, and Well-Being. The interconnection between SDG9 and SDG3 in the context of infrastructure policymaking is confirmed by Harris, Riley, Dawson, Friel, and Lawson (2020). Additionally, sustainability curriculum developers have coupled SDG9 with SDG4, quality education, and SDG16, peace, justice, and strong institutions (Chang & Lien, 2020).

All the above leads us to consider the strong interconnection between SDG9 and other SDGs as an enabling factor for leaving none behind. Responsible agencies for prompt reporting must determine where an initiative should be considered part of SDG9 or part of any other SDG. The good news is that SDGs are very complementary and mutually reinforcing, creating a ripple effect that maximises each other's benefits and harms.

2.4. WRAP UP

A wide range of insights about assessing progress towards the achievement of SDG9 was expressed in this chapter. However, a matter-of-fact analysis of the accuracy of the reports presented here is complicated because each one has a different approach to delivering information to promote a sustainable industry. Therefore, we have argued the utmost attention required to gather accurate and reliable U.N. reports, Voluntary National Reviews, and unofficial sustainability reports. In addition, most member states collect data through National Statistical Systems from environmental agencies and other agencies related to infrastructure and urban development, digital communications, and patent and trademark office. The difficulty of obtaining accurate quality data stems from the diversity of federal official data sources. Therefore, generating insights about assessing progress towards SDG9 was like piecing together a puzzle. Unfortunately, SDG reports are characterised as descriptive in content with few quantitative indicators. This insight might explain why the achievements and results on SDG9 are often estimates, scarce, and aggregate.

REFERENCES

Allen, C., Metternicht, G., & Wiedmann, T. (2018). Initial progress in implementing the Sustainable Development Goals (SDGs): A review of evidence from countries. *Sustainability Science*, *13*(5), 1453–1467. doi:10.1007/s11625-018-0572-3

Allen, C., Metternicht, G., & Wiedmann, T. (2019). Prioritising SDG targets: Assessing baselines, gaps and interlinkages. *Sustainability Science*, *14*(2), 421–438. doi:10.1007/s11625-018-0596-8

Allen, C., Nejdawi, R., El-Baba, J., Hamati, K., Metternicht, G., & Wiedmann, T. (2017). Indicator-based assessments of progress towards the sustainable development goals (SDGs): A case study from the Arab region. *Sustainability Science*, *12*(6), 975–989. doi:10.1007/s11625-017-0437-1

Allen, C., Reid, M., Thwaites, J., Glover, R., & Kestin, T. (2020). Assessing national progress and priorities for the Sustainable Development Goals (SDGs): Experience from Australia. *Sustainability Science*, *15*(2), 521–538. doi:10.1007/s11625-019-00711-x

Bell, S., & Morse, S. (2018). Sustainability indicators past and present: What next? *Sustainability (Switzerland)*, *10*(5), 1–15. doi:10.3390/su10051688

Business and Industry Major Group. (2017). *Realizing the potential of the private sector to eradicate poverty and promote prosperity in a changing world*. Position Paper for HLPF, 1–6. Retrieved from https://sustainabledevelopment.un.org/content/documents/14934BIMGSectoralPositionPaper.pdf. Accessed on April 27, 2021.

Chang, Y.-C., & Lien, H.-L. (2020). Mapping course sustainability by embedding the SDGs inventory into the university curriculum: A case study from National University of Kaohsiung in Taiwan. *Sustainability*, *12*(10), 4274. MDPI AG. doi:10.3390/su12104274

De Oliveira, A., & Kindornay, S. (2021). *Progressing National SDG Implementation: An independent assessment of the voluntary national review reports submitted to the United Nations High-level Political Forum in 2020*. Ottawa: Cooperation Canada.

Garrett, R., & Latawiec, A. E. (2015). What are sustainability indicators for? In M. Golachowska-Poleszczuk & A.

Topoloska (Eds.), *Sustainability indicators in practice* (pp. 12–22). Warsaw/Berlin: De Gruyter Open Ltd.

Gromek, P., & Sobolewski, G. (2020). Risk-based approach for informing sustainable infrastructure resilience enhancement and potential resilience implication in terms of emergency service perspective. *Sustainability (Switzerland)*, *12*(11), 1–30. doi:10.3390/su12114530

Harris, P., Riley, E., Dawson, A., Friel, S., & Lawson, K. (2020). Stop Talking around projects and talk about solutions: Positioning health within infrastructure policy to achieve the sustainable developments goals. *Health Polity*, *124*(6), 591–598. doi:10.1016/j.healthpol.2018.11.013

HLPF. (2017). President's Summary of 2017 high-level political forum on sustainable development. *High-Level Political Forum on Sustainable Development*, 1–13. Retrieved from https://sustainabledevelopment.un.org/hlpf/2017. Accessed on April 25, 2021.

Hoek, M. (2018). The trillion dollar shift achieving the sustainable development goals: Business for good is good business. In A. de Jeu (Ed.), *The trillion dollar shift* (First published). New York, NY: Routledge. doi:10.4324/9781351107297

Horan, D. (2020). National baselines for integrated implementation of an environmental sustainable development goal assessed in a new integrated SDG index. *Sustainability (Switzerland)*, *12*(17), 1–22. doi:10.3390/SU12176955

Huatuco, L. H., & Ball, P. D. (2019). The quest for achieving United Nations sustainable development goals (SDGs): Infrastructure and innovation for responsible production and consumption. *RAUSP Management Journal*, *54*(3), 357–362. doi:10.1108/RAUSP-04-2019-0068

IISD. (2021). Goal 9 – Industry, innovation & infrastructure. Retrieved from http://sdg.iisd.org/sdgs/goal-9-industry-innovation-infrastructure/. Accessed on May 17, 2021.

Ilie, C. M., Brovelli, M. A., & Coetzee, S. (2019). Monitoring SDG9 with global open data and open software: A case study from rural Tanzania. *International Archives of the Photogrammetry, Remote Sensing and Spatial Information Sciences - ISPRS Archives*, 42(2/W13), 1551–1558. doi:10.5194/isprs-archives-XLII-2-W13-1551-2019

Kunčič, A. (2018). SDG-specific country groups: Subregional analysis of the Arab Region. *Review of Middle East Economics and Finance*, 14(2). doi:10.1515/rmeef-2017-0020

Labbate, R., Silva, R. F., Rampasso, I. S., Anholon, R., Quelhas, O. L. G., & Leal Filho, W. (2021). Business models towards SDGs: The barriers for operationalizing Product-Service System (PSS) in Brazil. *International Journal of Sustainable Development and World Ecology*, 28(4), 350–359. doi:10.1080/13504509.2020.1823517

Lillehagen, I., Heggen, K. M., Tomson, G., & Engebretsen, E. (2020). Implementing the U.N. sustainable development goals: How is health framed in the Norwegian and Swedish voluntary national review reports? *International Journal of Health Policy and Management*, x, 1–10. doi:10.34172/ijhpm.2020.221

Obersteiner, M., Walsh, B., Frank, S., Havlík, P., Cantele, M., Liu, J., … Van Vuuren, D. (2016). Assessing the land resource–food price nexus of the Sustainable Development Goals. *Science Advances*, 2(9). doi:10.1126/sciadv.1501499

Reid, J., & Rout, M. (2020). Developing sustainability indicators – The need for radical transparency. *Ecological Indicators*, 110(June 2019). doi:10.1016/j.ecolind.2019.105941

Rosado-González, E. M., Palacio-Prieto, J. L., & Abreu-Sá, A. A. (2020). Geotourism in Latin America and Caribbean UNESCO global geoparks: Contribution for sustainable development goals. In V. Ratten (Ed.), *Technological progress, inequality and entrepreneurship. Studies on entrepreneurship, structural change, and industrial dynamics*. Cham: Springer. doi:10.1007/978-3-030-26245-7_7

Sachs, J., Schmidt-Traub, G., Kroll, C., Lafortune, G., Fuller, G., Woelm, F. (2020). *Sustainable Development Report 2020. The Sustainable Development Goals and COVID-19*. Cambridge: Cambridge University Press. Retrieved from https://s3.amazonaws.com/sustainabledevelopment. report/2020/2020_sustainable_development_report.pdf. Accessed on March 25, 2021.

Scheyvens, R., Banks, G., & Hughes, E. (2016). The private sector and the SDGs: The need to move beyond 'business as usual'. *Sustainable Development*, 24(6), 371–382. doi:10.1002/sd.1623

Sinha, A., Sengupta, T., & Alvarado, R. (2020). Interplay between technological innovation and environmental quality: Formulating the SDG policies for next 11 economies. *Journal of Cleaner Production*, 242, 118549. doi:10.1016/j. jclepro.2019.118549

U.N. Economic and Social Council. (2017). Ministerial declaration of the high-level segment of the 2017 session of the Economic and Social Council on the annual theme "Eradicating poverty in all its forms and dimensions through promoting sustainable development, expanding opportunities and address, 1–10. Retrieved from https://undocs.org/ pdf?symbol=es/E/HLS/2017/1. Accessed on May 12, 2021.

U.N. Global Compact. (2020). *Uniting business in the decade of action – Building on 20 Years of Progress*. Retrieved from https://globalcompact.no/wp-content/uploads/2020/06/publikasjon.pdf. Accessed on May 9, 2021.

U.N. Global compact. (2021b). *Activities to support advancing the SDGs from all reporting companies*. Retrieved from https://www.unglobalcompact.org/interactive/sdgs/global. Accessed on March 25, 2021.

UCLG. (2020). *Towards the localization of the SDGs: How to accelerate transformative actions in the aftermath of the COVID-19 outbreak*. Retrieved from http://www.agenda2030.oaxaca.gob.mx/wp-content/uploads/2020/07/4.-report_localization_hlpf_2020.pdf. Accessed on May 15, 2021.

UN Committee for Development Policy. (2021). *The 2020 VNRs: points for reflection in preparation for the 2021 reviews* (Issue April). Retrieved from https://www.un.org/development/desa/dpad/wp-content/uploads/sites/45/CDP-Reflections-2021-VNRs.pdf. Accessed on March 25, 2021.

United Nations. (2020). The Sustainable Development Goals. In *The Sustainable Development Goals Report 2020*. Retrieved from The-Sustainable-Development-Goals-Report-2020.pdf (un.org). Accessed on March 27, 2021.

United Nations Department of Economic and Social Affairs (UN DESA). (2019). Good practices, success stories and lessons learned in SDG Implementation. In *Sustainable Development Knowledge Platform* (Issue March 2020). Retrieved from https://sustainabledevelopment.un.org/sdgs/goodpractices. Accessed on March 27, 2021

WBCSD. (2021). *Vision 2050 – Time to Transform*. Retrieved from https://www.wbcsd.org/Overview/About-us/Vision-2050-Refresh/Resources/Time-to-Transform. Accessed on April 25, 2021.

4

U.N. DECADE OF ACTION

ABSTRACT

In resolution A/RES/74/4, the U.N. Nations General Assembly adopted the Decade of Action to accelerate the achievement of the SDGs by 2030. The Decade of Action calls to improve actual efforts to accomplish the 2030 agenda for governments, civil society, the private sector, and other stakeholders. This call is the last opportunity we have to reach SDG9. Still, unfortunately, the COVID-19 pandemic has severely affected all industrial sectors, which is unlikely to achieve inclusive and sustainable industrialisation by 2030. This chapter illustrates the adverse effects that the construction, manufacturing, and hospitality industries have suffered since the beginning of the COVID-19 pandemic and how they gradually have returned to the new normal. It also shows the case of the industry that could be considered the 'champion in the covid era', the high-tech industry. Predominantly in covid times, high-tech firms have been a synonym for technological innovation, which is an absolute necessity to encourage competitiveness in all industrial sectors, mainly in essential activities. Finally, the chapter is closed with an invitation to reflect on the fundamental principle of SDG9, which is sustainable industrialisation, but above all, inclusivity. SDG9 cannot be considered achieved until its benefits are transferred to the countries in the global south.

Keywords: Decade of action; SDG9 progress; COVID-19; construction; manufacturing; hospitality; high-tech; industry

1.1. WHAT IS THE DECADE OF ACTION?

In October 2019, the General Assembly adopted the political declaration of the high-level political forum on sustainable development by resolution A/RES/74/4. The statement refers to the achievements and shortcomings of member states in meeting the SDG in the 2030 Agenda. As a strategic measure to address those shortcomings and speed out the progress towards the implementation of the SDGs, a decade of actions, starting in 2020, was adopted. The provisions of the fourth paragraph state:

> *Today, we are launching an ambitious and accelerated response to reach our common vision by 2030 and pledging to make the coming decade one of action and delivery. We will maintain the integrity of the 2030 Agenda, including by ensuring ambitious and continuous action on the targets of the Sustainable Development Goals with a 2020 timeline. (UN-General Assembly, 2019)*

The declaration ends endorsing the need to carry out corrective actions to comply with the commitments established in the 2030 Agenda during the present decade.

> *We know the world we want. We pledge to accelerate our common efforts now and in the coming decade, to reach this vision by 2030. Rapid change is possible, and the Goals remain within reach if we embrace transformation and accelerate implementation. (UN-General Assembly, 2019)*

In this context, the U.N. Department of Economic and Social Affairs established the SDG Acceleration Actions project to gather voluntarily undertaken initiatives to expedite SDG implementation by national governments and other non-state actors, individually or in partnership. As of February 2020, a total of 147 acceleration actions have been published, mainly focussed on SDGs 16, 17, 13, 8, 5, and 1. Concerning SDG9, 40 initiatives were registered (UN DESA, 2020). Unfortunately, the decade of actions had the worst possible start imaginable. The initial assessment in the 2020 Sustainable Development Goals Report was not encouraging. As discussed in the previous chapter, the United Nations Department of Economic and Social Affairs recognised that there is no guarantee in any way that the goals will be met by 2030. Therefore, the report proposes more vigorous efforts to improve the situation of the least developed countries since their current level of progress is far from being what was initially forecast (United Nations, 2020).

As if this were not enough, the COVID-19 pandemic created an unprecedented scenario for the worldwide industry as never before. From supply chain to marketing, the pandemic exacerbated conditions in almost the full range of activities needed to create a product or service within the domain of SDG9. Today, the extent of the industry affectations remains unknown, but it is undeniable that COVID-19 has reversed the progress on of SDG9. Except for a few specific cases, most industries are at risk of stopping operations due to this pandemic (Daily Telegraph, 2020; Schwimmer, 2020). Nevertheless on the other hand, questioning the actual status quo mindset for sustainability requires an extraordinary agent of change; after all, this is not the first time disasters or economic crises force societies to adapt to a new reality (Chirot, 2012, Chapter 5).

The pandemic has made us lose almost two years of the decade of action, but not all is lost. Before the pandemic, many industrial firms had managed to advance towards SDG9; perhaps those achievements will help build resilience against the disruptions of COVID. The following sections of this chapter show the effect of the pandemic in crucial industrial sectors to achieve the objective and how they have managed to restart their activities.

1.2. THE CONSTRUCTION INDUSTRY (CI)

The CI entails meaningful links to SDG9, specifically 9.1, 9.4, and 9.a. The pledge of 'leave no one behind' demands infrastructure investment for rural development and mainly in the least developed countries, where the lack of basic infrastructure is a more significant impediment for economic growth and provides an acceptable quality of life to everyone (International Labour Organization (ILO), 2019). With a share of more than 6% of the global Gross Domestic Product (GDP) (World Economic Forum (WEF), 2016) and the generation of more than 100 million direct and indirect jobs worldwide (Deloitte Spain, 2019), construction is one of the most critical drives for the world economy.

Unfortunately, the CI has been one of the economic sectors most affected by the COVID-19 pandemic, which is extremely serious for the world economy. A 2020 survey conducted by the Associated General Contractors of America (AGC, 2020) reveals severe disruptions to the CI in the United States of America, such as the halt, delay, and cancellation of projects.

The pandemic has affected the whole CI; the extent of the impact has been more significant in more vulnerable persons. According to the OECD (2021), the economic consequences derived from the pandemic have had more profound financial repercussions in Small and medium-sized enterprises (SMEs) than in larger firms. Nevertheless, the pandemic threatens all SMEs; those that have managed to survive showed organisational characteristics that favourably influenced the handling of the crisis, such as workforce, annual turnover, and total assets (Alara, 2021).

Regarding the construction labour force, it is characterised by older workers, Hispanics, afro-Americans. This segment of workers often presents underlying medical conditions or other risk factors; and, consequently, a greater risk of getting seriously ill. A socio-demographic structure analytical study of the construction workforce suggests that workers in the CI are at greater risk of suffering from the COVID-19 virus than workers in other industries. The study concluded that nearly 6 in 10 workers, 59.4%, had a least one condition associated with a higher risk of severe illness from COVID-19 (Brown, Brooks, & Dong, 2020).

Even though it is impossible to predict with certainty how quickly the CI will fully recover from the pandemic, there are currently good signs suggesting a long-term recovery. In the meantime, it is necessary to implement anti-covid measures in construction work centres. Unlike other professions, the workforce in the CI cannot perform virtual working; therefore, as the construction workers return to the new normal, they will need to get used to new working conditions, even doing the same tasks. In this sense, the ILO proposes an action checklist for the CI that includes 48 practical measures to prevent and mitigate the spread of COVID-19 at work centres, grouped in the following four themes (ILO, 2020).

I.   Policy, planning, and organisation,
II. Risk assessment, management, and communication,
III. Prevention and mitigation measures,
IV. Arrangements for health surveillance and the identification and monitoring of suspected and confirmed COVID-19 cases.

In light of the unprecedented pandemic, the CI requires to scale up investment in climate-resilient infrastructure. However, in doing so, most construction firms could go bankrupt without government help. Considering the economic role of this industry, governments should provide support them to maintain their operations and workforce by implementing strategies that allow them to build resilient capacity.

1.3. THE MANUFACTURING INDUSTRY (MI)

The MI ideally incorporates the principles of SDG9; however, it is involved with specific targets 9.4, 9.5. Furthermore, it is an excellent example of the indivisibility, integration, and interconnectedness among all SDGs. During the first months of the COVID-19 pandemic, worldwide lockdowns have severely hit manufacturing, not surprisingly, due to changes in household consumption patterns (Blundell, Griffith, Levell, & O'Connell, 2020). First of all, the widespread fear of COVID-19's consequences raised concerns about food and sanitary goods scarcity, which led shoppers to queue outside stores to buy for stockpiling (Naeem, 2020). After acquiring the basics, shoppers opted to be more cautious, forgetting to buy unnecessary or luxury items (Hobbs, 2020; Mehta, Saxena, & Purohit, 2020; Tuncer, 2020). Then, it came mobility restrictions, which had a significant impact on global oil demand.

Demand plummeted to the point that there was no place to store the global crude production, provoking the price of the leading US oil benchmark to fall below zero. In this scenario, the Organization of the Petroleum Exporting Countries forecasted a historical decline of 6.8 million barrels per day (OPEC, 2020). Supply chains suffered severely from the change in consumer's consumption behaviours. For instance, the demand for medical-related products soared, resulting in temporary technical difficulties in production lines and out-of-stock items in stores (Anholon & Rampasso, 2020). Agricultural and food industries' supply chains were also disrupted by current consumption patterns (Kerr, 2020). This supply chain is sensitive to sudden changes in demand since products cannot remain in silos long before being processed. On the other hand, it is also impossible to suddenly increase the harvested volume of food products.

During this period, suppliers' capacity to deliver was surpassed for many fresh food products (Hao, Wang, & Zhou, 2020). As the industry adapted to chaos in supply chains, the price of products increased (Guo, Liu, Shi, & Chen, 2020). It is expected that while the pandemic lasts, more disruptions in supply chains and across industries are likely to occur (Free & Hecimovic, 2020). However, the overall effects will be transitory from an economic approach (Wang, Wang, & Wang, 2020). In this sense, online shopping has become a mitigation measure to *leverage* the economy and increase consumer shopping desire (Briggs, Ellis, Lloyd, & Telford, 2020; Sharma & Jhamb, 2020). While the tragedy worsened for the economic and social dimensions of sustainability, the situation improved significantly for the environmental dimension. The slowdown in the global economy caused the flow of matter and energy in global supply chains to slow down (Schaltegger, 2020). In other words, for a short period, conservation of natural resources was favoured, and less energy was required by production processes, just as the scholars of strong sustainability advocated (Costanza & Daly, 1992; Beckerman, 1995; Voget-Kleschin, 2013). At that time, estimations verified that reductions in primary NOx, SOx, NMVOCs emissions originated from the most severe COVID-19 lockdown periods in Europe (Guevara et al., 2021), the United States of America (Freedman & Tierney, 2020), and China (Myllyvirta, 2020).

Furthermore, the National Center for Environmental Information (NCEI) notes a broader spectrum of environmental benefits, including cleaner air and respites for wildlife reducing vehicle traffic, air travel, shipping manufacturing, and other activities (NOAA News, 2019). Collectively, no world event in the twentieth century to date has produced more significant decreases in emissions (Quéré et al., 2020). However, the decarbonisation of the economy did not prevent millions who lost their jobs affecting the household economy (Duffin, 2020). As a response, many governments took measures to support financial stability and avoid the closure of businesses, such as adopting massive relief packages (Kimura, Thangavelu, Narjoko, & Findlay, 2020) and implementing a more relaxed regulatory enforcement on pollution emissions generated by the MI (Chang, Zhang, Paczkowski, Kohler, & Ribeiro, 2021). Today, there are encouraging signs of economic recovery as the growth of retail sales and all economic activity has enhanced industrial output (Telford, 2020). Still, environmental improvements have been fading as the industry has returned to normal.

The COVID-19 developments highlighted the unsustainability of our current system. However, it also remarked opportunities for industry to build new skills and to re-engineer current globalised systems of production that are based on complex, environmentally unfriendly value chains and the international shipment of billions of components. Industry stakeholders have scrutinised the ability to assess the feasibility of achieving SDG9, and the whole U.N.'s 2030 Agenda to shift away from energy-intensive forms of transportation and achieve more sustainable industrialisation, due to the change in consumption patterns during the pandemic.

The Hospitality Industry (H.I.)

This section covers two of the more critical sectors in the achievement of SDG9 in the hospitality industry: the aviation industry and tourism. They have also been one of the most negatively impacted by COVID-19. Without explicitly referring to SDG9, scientific literature about the aforementioned sectors often refers to resilient infrastructure, information and communication technologies (ICTs), and innovation, previously debated in Chapter 1. Exceptionally, it is possible to find in the literature manuscripts that explicitly refer to the hospitality sector concerning SDG9 (Spencer & McBean, 2020). Still, it should be understood that both the aviation industry and tourism require an infrastructure that is resilient to the impacts of climate change and global warming. Also, both rely on ICTs to perform high-efficiency functions. Additionally, innovation is one of the strongest drivers to increase corporate sustainability in the aviation industry, which is highly committed to reducing its primary pollutants associated with global air quality and human health impacts (Dedoussi, 2021).

In the wake of the COVID-19 pandemic, the aviation industry suffered one of its worst crises, if not the worst, in its entire history. Traveller preferences have changed due to the pandemic. Today, many more people prefer domestic destinations, make short flights (Schumann, 2021). Consequently, airlines face a substantial increase in stock market volatility (Liu et al., 2020). Furthermore, although the estimated risk of being infected with SARS-CoV-2 during a commercial flight is relatively low, people preferred to travel by plane as minor as possible (Blomquist et al., 2021). Consequently, a severe drop in demand for airline services, primarily international flights, threatened the viability and profitability of many airlines (Forsyth, Guiomard, & Niemeier, 2020; Matiza, 2020).

Although air transportation's share of GDP is small, the COVID disruptions in this industry triggered negative economic repercussions in the whole aviation industry and other closely linked sectors (OECD, 2020). Among those, the tourism industry, which maintains a high share of GDP (Peña-Sánchez, Ruiz-Chico, Jiménez-García, & López-Sánchez, 2020). However, it has been severely affected by the pandemic (Dewi, 2020). On the other hand, the pandemic has also generated opportunities for improvement in tourism; for example, it has accelerated the digital transformation in the hospitality industry (Nuno & Paulo, 2021). For instance, the adoption of artificial intelligence tools for substituting tasks could risk staff health, although it is still too early to evaluate the measures implemented (Li, Yin, Qiu, & Bai, 2021).

Furthermore, in the post-COVID-19 era, innovative technologies allowed the creation of never before imagined services such as virtual tourism. Virtual tourism is an attractive alternative to know tourist places from home (Akhtar et al., 2021). Undoubtedly, few sectors have been affected as hard as the hospitality industry, particularly the air transportation sector, which has created a domino effect on other companies. However, the pandemic might bring positive changes to the industry, such as adopting digital technology to better service to guests.

1.4. HIGH-TECH INDUSTRY

More than a year and a half after the World Health Organization declared the pandemic's start, the industry has resumed its operations within what is considered the new normal. This unpredictable event brought significant negative impacts on the performance of thousands of firms. Counting the damages implies acknowledging that many businesses could not bear the lockdown consequences for the vast majority. Still, many more became more resilient than previously thought and restarted operations. An exceptional case has been the experience of the high-tech giants that while COVID-19 turned out to be the worst nightmare in many industrial sectors, the high-tech industry was experiencing bonanza times. The fight against covid-19 created unimaginable niches for high technology adoption in all industrial sectors (He, Sun, Zhang, & Li, 2020).

Healthcare technology companies deserve special attention. Since decades ago, ICT in the healthcare industry has constantly assisted health care workers, patients, and authorities in generating patient data for diagnostic decision-making, treatment of diseases, surgical procedures, and administrative tasks (Yelton & Schoener, 2020). During the pandemic, health care technology such as intelligent robotics, autonomous systems, and intelligent wearables has been deployed to facilitate the prevention, containment, and mitigation of COVID-19 (Tavakoli, Carriere, & Torabi, 2020). They became essential for providing a wide range of services such as infection detection, travel history analysis, identification of infection symptoms, early detection, transmission identification, access to information in lockdown, movement of people, and developing medical treatments and vaccines (Alshammari et al., 2021).

Here the question continues to be concerning the inclusiveness and sustainability of medical services. Do the most vulnerable have access to this wide range of medical services or only the wealthy? This question does not have a direct answer, and it may be different in each country. Since before the pandemic, there have been records indicating the difficulties of developing countries in managing health technologies effectively (Houngbo et al., 2017). Some argue that adopting technologies in the health services sector is not enough to avoid the disparities inherent in the capitalist health care system; instead, it feeds and exacerbates the inequities of the market economy by letting tech giants profiting from the pandemic (Yeo, 2021).

The manufacture and worldwide distribution of vaccines against covid-19 is a clear example of the inequity in health services between global north countries and those in the global south. The situation in the health industry is an excellent example to illustrate the purpose of SDG9, which is aimed not only at increasing resilient infrastructure, innovating industrial processes and services, and increasing the logistics provided by ICT. All of this will be of little use if these factors cannot be transferred to countries in the global south.

1.5. WRAP UP

The momentum of the decade of action faded entirely in most SDGs because of the emergence of COVID-19. As we learned in this chapter, industries related to ICTs and innovation have flourished during the pandemic and are likely to continue to strengthen. Conversely, many other industries have suffered seriously from the consequences of the pandemic. The examples that we have seen in the section may be the most representative of the industry, but they are not the only ones. We have less than 10 years to achieve inclusive and sustainable industrialisation. SDG9 will not be achieved without the sum of efforts of all interest groups. Government, Industry, and Civil Society.

REFERENCES

AGC. (2020). *AGC Coronavirus Survey Results (June 9–17)*. Associated General Contractors of America. Retrieved from https://www.agc.org/coronavirus/agc-surveys. Accessed on June 05, 2021.

Akhtar, N., Khan, N., Mahroof Khan, M., Ashraf, S., Hashmi, M. S., Khan, M. M., & Hishan, S. S. (2021). Post-COVID 19 tourism: Will digital tourism replace mass tourism? *Sustainability*, *13*(10), 5352. doi:10.3390/su13105352

Alara, S. A. (2021). Organizational characteristics and COVID-19 safety practices among small and medium construction enterprises (SMEs) in Nigeria. *Frontiers in Engineering and Built Environment*, ahead of print. doi:10.1108/FEBE-02-2021-0006

Alshammari, N., Sarker, M. N. I., Kamruzzaman, M. M., Alruwaili, M., Alanazi, S. A., Raihan, M. L., & AlQahtani, S. A. (2021). Technology-driven 5G enabled e-healthcare system during COVID-19 pandemic. *IET Communications, May*, 1–15. doi:10.1049/cmu2.12240

Anholon, R., & Rampasso, I. S. (2020). The COVID-19 pandemic and the growing need to train engineers aligned to the sustainable development goals. *International Journal of Sustainability in Higher Education*, *21*(6), 1269–1275. doi:10.1108/IJSHE-06-2020-0217

Beckerman, W. (1995). How would you like your sustainability, sir? Weak or strong? A reply to my critics. *Environmental Values*, *4*(2), 169–179. Retrieved from www.jstor.org/stable/30301474. Accessed on May 05, 2020.

Blomquist, P. B., Bolt, H., Packer, S., Schaefer, U., Platt, S., Dabrera, G., Gobin, M., & Oliver, I. (2021). Risk of symptomatic COVID-19 due to aircraft transmission: A retrospective cohort study of contact-traced flights during England's containment phase. *Influenza and Other Respiratory Viruses*, *15*(3), 336–344. doi:10.1111/irv.12846

Blundell, R., Griffith, R., Levell, P., & O'Connell, M. (2020). Could COVID-19 infect the consumer prices index? *Fiscal Studies*, *41*(2), 357–361. doi:10.1111/1475-5890.12229

Briggs, D., Ellis, A., Lloyd, A., & Telford, L. (2020). New hope or old futures in disguise? Neoliberalism, the Covid-19 pandemic and the possibility for social change. *International Journal of Sociology and Social Policy*. In press. doi:10.1108/IJSSP-07-2020-0268

Brown, S., Brooks, R. D., & Dong, X. S. (2020). Coronavirus and Health Disparities in Construction. *CPWR*. Retrieved from https://www.cpwr.com/wp-content/uploads/publications/DataBulletin-May2020.pdf. Accessed on June 06, 2021.

Chang, E., Zhang, K., Paczkowski, M., Kohler, S., & Ribeiro, M. (2021). Association of temporary Environmental Protection Agency regulation suspension with industrial economic viability and local air quality in California, United States. *Environmental Sciences Europe*, *33*(1). doi:10.1186/s12302-021-00489-9

Chirot, D. (2012). Toward a theory of social change. In *How societies change* [Internet] (2nd ed., pp. 129–145). SAGE-PINE FORGE. Retrieved from https://us.sagepub.com/en-us/nam/how-societies-change/book235597

Costanza, R., & Daly, H. (1992). Natural capital and sustainable development. *Conservation Biology* [Internet], 6(1), 37–46. Retrieved from http://links.jstor.org/sici?sici=0888-8892%28199203%296%3A1%3C37%3ANCASD%3E2.0.C=%3B2-M

Daily Telegraph. (2020). *Winners and losers: How burden of Covid spared some entrepreneurs before others* [London, England], December 18 2020, p. 8. Gale OneFile: News, link. gale.com/apps/doc/A645463219/STND?u=purchase&sid=STND&xid=49d1fc52. Accessed on March 23, 2021.

Dedoussi, I. C. (2021). Implications of future atmospheric composition in decision-making for sustainable aviation. *Environmental Research Letters*, 16(3). doi:10.1088/1748-9326/abe74d

Deloitte Spain. (2019). *Global Power of Construction 2018*. Retrieved from https://www2.deloitte.com/content/dam/Deloitte/at/Documents/presse/Deloitte-Global-Powers-of-Construction-2019.pdf%0Ahttps://www2.deloitte.com/content/dam/Deloitte/at/Documents/real-estate/2017-global-powers-of-construction.pdf. Accessed on June 05, 2021.

Dewi, L. (2020). Resilience Ecotourism in Papua Amid Covid 19 Pandemic. *E-Journal of Tourism*, 7(2), 250. doi:10.24922/eot.v7i2.61831

Duffin, E. (2020). Impact of the coronavirus pandemic on the global economy – Statistics & Facts o Title. Retrieved from https://www.statista.com/topics/6139/covid-19-impact-on-the-global-economy/. Accessed on December 10, 2020.

Forsyth, P., Guiomard, P., & Niemeier, H. M. (2020). Covid-19, the collapse in passenger demand and airport charges. *Journal of Air Transport Management*, 89, In press. doi:10.1016/j.jairtraman.2020.101932

Free, C., & Hecimovic, A. (2020). Global supply chains after COVID-19: The end of the road for neoliberal globalisation? *Accounting, Auditing & Accountability Journal*. In press. doi:10.1108/AAAJ-06-2020-4634

Freedman, A., & Tierney, L. (2020). The silver lining to coronavirus lockdowns: Air quality is improving. *Washington Post* [Internet]. Retrieved from https://www.washingtonpost.com/weather/2020/04/09/air-quality-improving-coronavirus/

Guevara, M., Jorba, O., Soret, A., Petetin, H., Bowdalo, D., Serradell, K., … Pérez Garciá-Pando, C. (2021). Time-resolved emission reductions for atmospheric chemistry modelling in Europe during the COVID-19 lockdowns. *Atmospheric Chemistry and Physics*, *21*(2), 773–797. doi:10.5194/acp-21-773-2021

Guo, H., Liu, Y., Shi, X., & Chen, K. Z. (2020). The role of E-commerce in the urban food system under COVID-19: Lessons from China. *China Agricultural Economic Review*. In press. doi:10.1108/CAER-06-2020-0146

Hao, N., Wang, H. H., & Zhou, Q. (2020). The impact of online grocery shopping on stockpile behavior in Covid-19. China Agricultural Economic Review, *12*(3), 459–470. doi:10.1108/CAER-04-2020-0064

He, P., Sun, Y., Zhang, Y., & Li, T. (2020). COVID-19's impact on stock prices across different sectors: An event study based on the Chinese Stock Market. *Emerging Markets Finance and Trade*, *56*(10), 2198–2212. doi:10.1080/1540496X.2020.1785865

Hobbs, J. E. (2020). Food supply chains during the COVID-19 pandemic. *Canadian Journal of Agricultural Economics*, *68*(April), 171–176. doi:10.1111/cjag.12237

Houngbo, P. T., Buning, T. de C., Bunders, J., Coleman, H. L., Medenou, D., Dakpanon, L., & Zweekhorst, M. (2017). Ineffective healthcare technology management in Benin's Public Health Sector: The perceptions of key actors and their ability to address the main problems. *International Journal of Health Policy and Management*, 6(10), 587–600. doi:10.15171/ijhpm.2017.17

International Labour Organization (ILO). (2019). *Developing the construction industry for employment-intensive infrastructure investments*. Retrieved from https://www.ilo.org/wcmsp5/groups/public/—ed_emp/—emp_policy/—invest/documents/publication/wcms_734235.pdf. Accessed on June 05, 2021.

International Labour Organization (ILO). (2020). *COVID-19 action checklist for the construction industry. Practical measures to help employers, workers and the self-employer prevent and mitigate the transmission of COVID-19 in construction work*. Retrieved from https://www.ilo.org/global/topics/safety-and-health-at-work/resources-library/publications/WCMS_764847/lang-en/index.htm. Accessed on June 05, 2021.

Kerr, W. A. (2020). The COVID-19 pandemic and agriculture: Short- and long-run implications for international trade relations. *Canadian Journal of Agricultural Economics*, 68(April), 225–229. doi:10.1111/cjag.12230

Kimura, F., Thangavelu, S. M., Narjoko, D., & Findlay, C. (2020). Pandemic (COVID-19) policy, regional cooperation and the emerging global production network†. *Asian Economic Journal*, 34(1), 3–27. doi:10.1111/asej.12198

Li, M., Yin, D., Qiu, H., & Bai, B. (2021). Examining the effects of A.I. contactless services on customer psychological safety, perceived value, and hospitality service quality during the COVID-19 pandemic. *Journal of Hospitality Marketing & Management*, *00*(00), 1–25. doi:10.1080/19368623.2021.1934932

Liu, J., Qiao, P., Ding, J., Hankinson, L., Harriman, E. H., Schiller, E. M., Ramanauskaite, I., & Zhang, H. (2020). Will the aviation industry have a bright future after the COVID-19 Outbreak? Evidence from Chinese Airport Shipping Sector. *Journal of Risk and Financial Management*, *13*(11), 276. doi:10.3390/jrfm13110276

Matiza, T. (2020). Post-COVID-19 crisis travel behaviour: Towards mitigating the effects of perceived risk. *Journal of Tourism Futures*. In press. doi:10.1108/JTF-04-2020-0063

Mehta, S., Saxena, T., & Purohit, N. (2020). The new consumer behaviour paradigm amid COVID-19: Permanent or transient? *Journal of Health Management*, *22*(2), 291–301. doi:10.1177/0972063420940834

Myllyvirta, L. (2020). Analysis: Coronavirus temporarily reduced China's CO_2 emissions by a quarter. CarbonBrief [Internet]. United Kingdom. Retrieved from https://www.carbonbrief. org/analysis-coronavirus-has-temporarily-reduced-chinas-co2-emissions-by-a-quarter?utm_content=bufferae67b&utm_medium=social&utm_source=twitter.com&utm_campaign=buffer

Naeem, M. (2020). Understanding the customer psychology of impulse buying during COVID-19 pandemic: Implications for retailers. *International Journal of Retail & Distribution Management*. In press. doi:10.1108/IJRDM-08-2020-0317

NOAA. (2019). National Centers for Environmental Information, State of the Climate: Global Climate Report – Annual 2019 [Internet]. Retrieved from https://www.ncdc.noaa.gov/sotc/global/201913

Nuno, A., & Paulo, R. (2021). COVID 19: The catalyst for digital transformation in the hospitality industry? *Tourism Management Studies, 17*(2), 41–46. doi:10.18089/tms.2021.170204

OECD. (2020). *COVID-19 and the aviation industry: Impact and policy responses, OECD Policy Responses to Coronavirus (COVID-19)*. Paris: OECD Publishing. doi:10.1787/26d521c1-en. Accessed on June 18, 2021.

OECD. (2021). *One year of SME and entrepreneurship policy responses to COVID-19: Lessons learned to "build back better."* Retrieved from https://www.oecd.org/coronavirus/policy-responses/one-year-of-sme-and-entrepreneurship-policy-responses-to-covid-19-lessons-learned-to-build-back-better-9a230220/. Accessed on June 06, 2021.

OPEC. (2020). Monthly Oil Market Report [Internet]. Vienna Austria. Retrieved from https://momr.opec.org/pdf-download/

Peña-Sánchez, A. R., Ruiz-Chico, J., Jiménez-García, M., & López-Sánchez, J. A. (2020). Tourism and the SDGs: An analysis of economic growth, decent employment, and gender equality in the European Union (2009–2018). *Sustainability (Switzerland), 12*(13), 1–24. doi:10.3390/su12135480

Quere, C. L., Jackson, R. B., Jones, M. W., Smith, A. J. P., Abernethy, S., Andrew, R. M., De-Gol, A. J., Willis, D. R., Shan, Y., Canadell, J. G., Friedlingstein, P., Creutzig, F., & Peters, G. P. (2020). Temporary reduction in daily global CO2 emissions during the COVID-19 forced confinement. *Nature Climate Change, 10*(7), 647–653. https://doi.org/10.1038/s41558-020-0797-x

Schaltegger, S. (2020). Sustainability learnings from the COVID-19 crisis. Opportunities for resilient industry and business development. *Sustainability Accounting,*

Management and Policy Journal. In press. doi:10.1108/
SAMPJ-08-2020-0296

Schumann, F. R. (2021). Monitoring changes in resident attitudes
toward tourism development in small island destinations.
Journal of Global Tourism Research, 6(1), 61–66. doi:10.37020/
jgtr.6.1_61

Schwimmer, R. (2020). What's next After COVID?
Mergers and Acquisitions, 55(9), 1–23. Retrieved from
https://ezproxy.purchase.edu/login?qurl=https%3A%2F
%2Fwww.proquest.com%2Ftr%0Aade-journals%2Fwhats-
next-after-covid%2Fdocview%2F2455556816%2F
se-%0A2%3Faccountid%3D14171

Sharma, A., & Jhamb, D. (2020). Changing consumer
behaviours towards online shopping-an impact of Covid 19.
Academy of Marketing Studies Journal, 24(3), 2678.
Retrieved from https://www.proquest.com/openview/
54bb549f925f739f6f022e250ac937a3/1?cbl=38744&
pq-origsite=gscholar

Spencer, A. J., & McBean, L. M. (2020). Alignment of tourism
investment to the SDGs in Jamaica: An exploratory study.
Worldwide Hospitality and Tourism Themes, 12(3), 261–274.
doi:10.1108/WHATT-02-2020-0010

Tavakoli, M., Carriere, J., & Torabi, A. (2020). Robotics,
smart wearable technologies, and autonomous intelligent
systems for healthcare during the COVID-19 pandemic: An
analysis of the state of the art and future vision. *Advanced
Intelligent Systems*, 2(7), 1–7. doi:10.1002/aisy.202000071

Telford, T. (2020). Retail sales jump 7. 5% in June even as
new covid outbreaks stall reopenings. *The Washington Post,
July 16*. Retrieved from link.gale.com/apps/doc/A629632105/

AONE?u=purchase&sid=bookmark-AONE&xid=46fdc7ec. Accessed on June 7, 2021.

Tuncer, F. F. (2020). The spread of fear in the globalizing world: The case of COVID-19. *Journal of Public Affairs*, *20*(4), 1–9. doi:10.1002/pa.2162

UN DESA. (2020). *Information Brief on SDG Acceleration Actions*. 4–5. Retrieved form https://sustainabledevelopment. un.org/content/documents/25680Information_Brief_for_SDG_ Acceleration_Actions.pdf. Accessed on April 25, 2021.

UN-General Assembly. (2019). Political declaration of the high-level political forum on sustainable development convened under the auspices of the General Assembly, A/ RES/74/4. Retrieved from https://undocs.org/en/A/RES/74/4. Accessed on June 01, 2021.

United Nations. (2020). The Sustainable Development Goals. In *The Sustainable Development Goals Report 2020*. Retrieved from The-Sustainable-Development-Goals-Report-2020.pdf (un.org). Accessed on March 27, 2021.

Voget-Kleschin, L. (2013). Large-scale land acquisition: Evaluating its environmental aspects against the background of strong sustainability. *Journal of Agricultural and Environmental Ethics*, *26*, 1105–1126. doi:10.1007/ s10806-013-9448-9

Wang, Y., Wang, J., & Wang, X. (2020). COVID-19, supply chain disruption and China's Hog Market: A dynamic analysis. China Agricultural Economic Review, *12*(3), 427–443. doi:10.1108/CAER-04-2020-0053

World Economic Forum (WEF). (2016). *Shaping the future of construction: A breakthrough in mindset and technology* (Issue May). Retrieved from https://doi. org/10.1061/9780784402474. Accessed on June 05, 2021.

World Economic Forum (WEF). (2020). *COVID-19 risks outlook a preliminary mapping and its implications* (Issue May). Retrieved from https://www.weforum.org/reports/covid-19-risks-outlook-a-preliminary-mapping-and-its-implications. Accessed on June 05, 2021.

Yelton, S. J., & Schoener, B. (2020). The evolution of healthcare technology management in leading healthcare delivery organizations. *Biomedical Instrumentation and Technology, 54*(2), 119–124. doi:10.2345/0899-8205-54.2.119

Yeo, S. (2021). Tech companies and public health care in the ruins of COVID. *International Journal of Communication, 15*, 1617–1636. Retrieved from http:ijoc.org

BUILD BACK BETTER TOGETHER

The pandemic of COVID-19 is still ongoing at the time of writing this book, and it will continue to be a threat for a long time to the achievement of SDG9. The industry is striving to be resilient from the wide disruptions triggered by the COVID-19 crisis. How the future is likely to unfold cannot be predicted. However, there is much to do before the COVID-19 pandemic is a thing of the past. The goal is to return to the new normal with equality in each region of the planet. As vaccination increases, the industry is preparing to reconnect with suppliers and customers in a new normal. All industry sectors are putting the pieces back together by carrying out concrete measures to build resilience in the three sustainability dimensions as the best option to advance towards inclusion and sustainable industrialisation.

This pandemic, like all crises, will come to an end sooner or later. Then the economy will reactivate, and the industry will retake its course. So, let us not lose perspective and know that, although not everything is under our control, our attitude and decisions are. The current situation represents an opportunity for prioritising innovative workplace sustainability best practices to stop 'business as usual'. This situation encourages people to reflect on the fundamental principle of SDG9, which is sustainable industrialisation, but above all, inclusivity. SDG9 must not only aim to increase resilient infrastructure, innovate industrial processes and services, and increase the logistics provided by information and communication technology. Moreover, the benefits of SDG9 must be transferred to countries in the global south.

It is about 30 years since the United Nations Conference on Environment and Development, the Earth Summit, made a call to achieve Sustainable Development worldwide. This call has been repeated over the years, trying to reach more people without regard to race, colour, religion, or national origin. We all have learned something from COVID-19 that will help us avoid making the same mistakes we made in the past. The approach of Build Back Better Together has never been more appropriate than right now. Hopefully, COVID-19 will act as a catalyser that speeds up the progress towards Inclusive and Sustainable Industrial Development.

INDEX